Confident
Communication

This book is dedicated to Lisa, Christopher, and Ashley Parker
for always being there when the words would not come
and the dinner was getting cold.

Confident Communication

Speaking
Tips
for
Educators

Douglas A. Parker

CORWIN PRESS, INC.
A Sage Publications Company
Thousand Oaks, California

For information:

Corwin Press, Inc.
A Sage Publications Company
2455 Teller Road
Thousand Oaks, California 91320
www.corwinpress.com

Sage Publications Ltd.
6 Bonhill Street
London EC2A 4PU
United Kingdom

Sage Publications India Pvt. Ltd.
M-32 Market
Greater Kailash I
New Delhi 110 048 India

Printed in the United States of America

Library of Congress Cataloging-in-Publication Data

Parker, Douglas A., 1956-
Confident communication: Speaking tips for educators / by Douglas A. Parker.
    p. cm.
Includes bibliographical references and index.
ISBN 0-7619-4689-6 (cloth) — ISBN 0-7619-4690-X (pbk.)
    1. Communication in educationn—Handbooks, manuals, etc.
2. Public speaking—Handbooks, manuals, etc. I. Title.
LB1033.5 .P35 2003
808.5´1´02437—dc211
                                    2002007096

This book is printed on acid-free paper.

02 03 04 05 06 07 7 6 5 4 3 2 1

Acquisitions Editor:	Faye Zucker
Editorial Assistant:	Julia Parnell
Production Editor:	Olivia Weber
Typesetter:	C&M Digitals (P) Ltd
Indexer:	Pamela Van Huss
Cover Designer:	Michael Dubowe
Production Artist:	Michelle Lee

Contents

Preface

I shall speak forth my sentiments freely and without reserve.

—Patrick Henry, 1775

What exactly do you mean, I have to address the PTA tomorrow night?

—Douglas A. Parker, October 1981

Confident Communication: Speaking Tips for Educators is intended to be a comprehensive public-speaking resource for teachers, principals, and school administrators. As a concise learning tool, it can speak to educators at every level, addressing the critical affective aspects of learning how to speak in public.

My goals for this book and its readers include:

- Designing a resource exclusively for professional educators to use both in and out of the classroom
- Taking a skills-based, humanistic, and (whenever possible) humorous approach to the psychology and strategies that must be in place before a person can develop as a speaker
- Improving educators' confidence by slowly accentuating their essential speaking skills
- Emphasizing the educator's being aware of what is happening during a speech and how to develop hands-on strategies for taking control of the public-speaking process and its outcome

■ Employing unique, hands-on, webbing techniques for creating speeches

My training in developmental counseling and education and my 20 years of experience in educational administration, classroom teaching, and lecturing are the foundation underlying the positive speech conditioning (PSC) program described in this volume. Substantiated by the best current research available on learning styles and hands-on learning techniques, this book will, I hope, help educators overcome their natural fears of speaking in front of a group. You will develop the confidence you need for success by reading this book and applying its various techniques in your own educational settings.

ACKNOWLEDGMENTS

The author would like to recognize and thank Dr. John Holloran, Mr. Richard Rees, and Mrs. Patricia Webber for their skills and expertise in helping prepare this book.

Corwin Press would like to acknowledge the contributions of the following reviewers:

Cindy Knowles
   Trainer/Consultant
   Drug Prevention
   Dansville, NY

David Sidwell, Professor
   Department of Theatre Arts
   Utah State University
   Logan, UT

Donna Rollins
   Educator
   Dunnellon, FL

John Hranitz, Chairperson, Professor
   Department of Early Childhood Education and
      Elementary Education
   Bloomsburg University
   Bloomsburg, PA

About
the Author

Douglas A. Parker holds dual master's degrees in education and counseling. He is a lifelong educator who has dedicated himself to helping people learn how to communicate effectively. As a veteran teacher, coach, and administrator, he successfully coached his students in high school debate and speech teams, winning numerous local, state, national, and international titles using the same lessons and techniques that he brings to his public-speaking and English classes. In *Confident Communication: Speaking Tips for Educators*, he shares his experiences and classroom gifts with everyone who wants to discover public speaking from the thinking and feeling educator's point of view.

Introduction:
A Message
for Teachers,
Principals,
and School
Administrators

FILLING IN THE GAPS

As you progressed through your education courses in college, you gained more and more confidence that you could become a successful and dedicated educator someday. You learned how to construct tests, how to create rubrics, how to choose textbooks, how to manage your classrooms, and, in general, what to expect as a professional educator. As you signed your first employment contract, you believed that what you lacked in classroom familiarity you more than made up for in life experiences, bolstered by a substantial background in educational theory.

AND THEN ONE DAY,
THE CHILDREN WERE ALL YOURS

You quickly come to realize that there might have been some ever-so-slight gaps in what they taught you in college. You note

1

that your 13-year-old students have little or no respect for educational theory, and that classroom management does indeed mean raising your voice from time to time.

You also discover that you need to speak before various groups every now and then. *Wait a second—that wasn't in the job description!* Now you're sure that there were some gaps!

As a teacher, a principal, or a school administrator, you will be called on to make public speeches. However, no matter how long you have been on the job, and no matter what training you have had, you probably do not feel ready to make a speech. Even if you make speeches every day, you still could use a little help.

At best, you probably have had only one public-speaking course in college, and that was most likely designed to give you the maximum amount of speaking practice time with the minimum amount of training and instruction.

An essential philosophy guiding this book is that speaking in public should not be about sophisticated educational theory. Theory and research are based on established scientific principles; whereas public speaking is anything but reliable and valid. It involves real people talking about real issues in dynamic real-life situations.

What you need to survive as a professional teacher, principal, or school administrator in this millennium are both speaking opportunities and instructional support. The opportunities will be there for you, so what you really need now is the support. That's why you should keep this book close to you in your briefcase at all times. When a speaking event arises, you can refer quickly to this book for help in making decisions about what to say and how to say it. You are supported every step along the way, from writing the speech to answering questions after the presentation.

As the speaking opportunities continue, both your understanding of the dynamics involved in public speaking and your confidence in yourself as a speaker will flourish.

To put a very fine point on it, this book fills in the gaps and teaches you what they never taught you in college. So, with this resource tucked firmly away in your canvas briefcase, relax, keep your faith, and enjoy being a member of the finest profession on earth!

I

The Foundations of Speaking

1

Understanding Public Speaking

It All Began With Demosthenes

It all began back in 351 B.C. with an Athenian orator and public official by the name of **Demosthenes.** Despite the fact that he was born with a speech impediment, Demosthenes decided that he wanted to become the best public speaker of his time; so he packed up some supplies and sojourned to the Athenian woods. After pitching camp, he took to his task. While out jogging, he put several small Grecian pebbles in his mouth and began to recite some of his old speeches and verses.

At first, he sounded much as you would expect him to have sounded—like a fellow with rocks in his mouth. After a few weeks of practice, however, he began to sound "normal."

As you may have guessed by now, he spit out the Grecian pebbles and was all the better for the experience—the theory being that if he could speak normally with pebbles in his mouth, he would be that much better without them. Unfortunately, you cannot follow in Demosthenes' footsteps. First off, you will not be able to find any Grecian pebbles or Athenian woods unless you happen to live on that side of the ocean. In addition, you would lose many of your teacher friends if you walked around with rocks in your jaw. So what can you do?

Don't worry, public speaking will come to you. Since oratory was one of the three major studies of the Middle Ages' Seven Arts (along with logic and philosophy), you can still achieve classical skills in this modern age. Public speaking cannot be taught in a normal, lecturing kind of way; it is not something that you are born with; you can't even discover it in the normal sense by downloading it from the Internet—it must be experienced. You can learn only by doing. Think of this book as your road map to the experience of public speaking. Don't be afraid to grow.

Also, do not worry about the size of your audience (which, in the future, will often be referred to as the *speaking group* or the *listeners*). This program will work with two people or 200 people. Any veteran speaker will tell you that the size of the audience is not the issue—preparation is.

This book talks to developing and experienced educators who want to develop their skills in the most important life skill a person can have in the new millennium—the ability to stand up before a group of people and communicate a message.

Thinking. Planning. Communicating. These universal life skills appeal to everyone in all different countries and in different learning environments. The best way to reach your academic and professional goals is to stand up and express exactly what is on your mind. This book is on your side to reach those goals by helping you to obtain the skills needed to move forward.

Positive Speech Conditioning

This book uses a technique known as positive speech conditioning (PSC). PSC recognizes that you cannot just jump behind a podium and deliver a blood-stirring speech the first time at bat. Growth comes only from practice. A child does not spring up from her crib and run a 10K race. First, she learns to crawl, then walk, and then run. In the same manner, a child usually does not decide to abandon the idea of walking if she falls over a few times ("Sorry, Mom, I gave it a good shot."). You will gain confidence along the way because you'll have a solid base upon which to build.

DELIVERY STYLES

Before you begin, you should know about the various tactical-speaking delivery styles. Whether you are delivering a classroom speech or talking before your professional peers, you can decide which style is best for each speech when the time comes.

The three fundamental ways you can deliver a public speech are having your materials and notes in hand, memorizing your speech verbatim, or giving an **extemporaneous**—or off-the-cuff—speech. Certain situations call for different styles. For example, the formal speech before the board, which you have known about for some time, warrants either a memorized or a prompted speech; speaking off-the-cuff could appear disrespectful.

1. Materials in hand. Here you have your speech in front of you, either in a major outline form or word for word. The advantage is that it is hard to lose any material. The major disadvantage is that you cannot establish as much eye contact with the group.

2. Memorized. If you have the time to sit down and memorize a speech, you will be greatly rewarded in terms of group interaction. In Chapter 19, you will find memory enhancement tips and suggestions for interacting with an audience.

3. Extemporaneous speaking. Extemporized speeches are pretty much off-the-cuff. These are the most difficult speeches to deliver since you have to think on your feet, and unless you are very confident about your ability to synthesize information, process the data, and say it all in a normal, conversational tone, you may want to avoid this style as much as possible early on in your career. Of course, there are times when you simply must speak at a moment's notice, as you will discover in Chapter 13.

BASIC SPEECHES

The public-speaking lessons, skills, and suggestions are all embedded within certain settings inside and outside school, where teachers, principals, and school administrators represent themselves and their schools in the community. The table of contents reflects subtitles for some chapters, and these subtitles refer to the various educational settings and groups you might encounter as your speaking career develops (e.g., the first subtitle, which appears in Chapter 4, is "Assemblies and Other Large Groups of Students"). While these settings are offered as examples, this is not a comprehensive list. It is quite possible that you will be interested only in certain topics or skills. If that is the case, skip about the book and take from it what you need to be successful.

2

Forming a Speech Study Group

EXPERIENTIAL LEARNING AND PROCESSING (WHY YOU SHOULD FORM A SPEECH STUDY GROUP)

Recent brain-based research indicates that learning by experience alone is only a small part of the total learning process. While experience is valuable, you need to take time to review and process what happens with your friends and colleagues. Coaches have always known to break down each game for players on videotape or at the chalkboard to evaluate what happened and how to improve the next time out. A speech study group provides you with the opportunity to go over your last speaking event. While writing each draft, and after hearing each speech, your speech study group can assess your efforts so that you can take an honest look at your presentation at whatever stage, help you decide what you did well and what you need to improve, and guide your plans for your next trip to the podium. Speaking experiences help you become accustomed to public speaking, and processing your efforts with peers will help you to develop the confidence to communicate.

Forming a Speech Study Group

If possible, try to gather some of your colleagues together to form a **speech study group**. The goals of this group are to help each other write and **critique** speeches, to offer advice on speaking and presenting, and, in general, to act as a support group as each of you grows as a professional educator.

You as an individual can do a great deal to make sure that your speech study group floats, because a group is really only a collection of individuals. After all, as you grow with the group's help, so too will the group mature along with your help.

HELPING THE SPEAKER: OFFERING HONEST CRITICISM

Whether you find the time to practice your speeches with the group beforehand or if some of your colleagues sit in the audience as you speak, they can help you grow as a speaker by listening and commenting. One formal task of the group is to offer appropriate feedback to each speaker through formal and informal critiques. You will learn the appropriate techniques for critiquing at a later point; for now, you need to know only three formal rules for offering feedback to a speaker:

- Describe the speaker's mistakes—do not get personal.
- Be specific.
- Comment only on things the speaker can control, such as tone, content, or speed.

The speech study group has two basic roles while a member is speaking, one as a listener and one as an evaluator. Their responsibilities are outlined below.

As listeners:

- Do not judge the people by their speeches. Be genuine and sincere.
- Do not practice or think about your comments while the person is speaking.
- While the person is speaking, have a positive regard for the speaker.
- Try to understand speakers from their point of view.

As evaluators:

- Share feelings and thoughts with the speaker.
- Make "I" statements (e.g., "I think your speech was . . ." or "I feel you need to . . .")
- Be specific.
- Be constructive, not destructive.
- Remember that all speakers are unique—let them be themselves.
- Comment only on the speech—not on the speaker.
- Do not project your own biases onto the speech.

All the individuals in your group have their own thoughts, likes, dislikes, prejudices, and preconceptions. Sometimes communication becomes difficult in such a group, so it is important to realize from the start that it is okay to disagree with someone in the group. To disagree does not mean to become disagreeable. Rather, the even flow and exchange of ideas are most beneficial and can be hampered only by a disagreeable person.

To avoid any such problems, whatever you do as a member of a speech study group, when offering a critique, do not

- Offer clichés as real advice
- Drift off during the speech and then pretend to have all the right comments
- Try to show off by listing trivial concerns or nitpicking
- Make comments directed at the speaker's personality

Moreover, maybe the worst of all—do not let someone get away with a flawed speech. This proves that you do not care about the speaker's growth enough to take the personal risk of being honest. It is very difficult to develop trust within a group if everyone sweet-talks one another instead of employing genuine communication.

ACTIVE-LISTENING REQUIREMENTS

As listeners, you must take an active role in the process of communication. Active listeners not only hear what is said but also hear the hidden messages conveyed through **paralinguistics** (the way humans inflect words to produce certain meanings).

Studies show that the average listener will miss over 75% of the spoken message! The reason behind this is simple: The average speaker speaks at a rate of 130 to 170 words per minute, whereas the average listener's brain can comprehend over 400 words per minute. This means that the average brain starts to wander, since it becomes starved for stimulus. In short, your brain gets bored.

You must take special care that your brain does not shut down out of boredom, because even consciously interesting speeches can be subconsciously boring. To do this, you must concentrate physically on the speech and avoid all distractions, such as noises from a fan or other group members. You have to lock onto the speaker and the speech.

To accomplish active listening, you have to do the following:

- Hear the big message or speech-focusing statement (more about this in Chapter 3) as quickly as possible
- Maintain a positive regard for the speaker
- Not become defensive or tune out if you hear something that you do not like
- Not judge the speaker during the speech
- Observe the speaker's body language and the paralinguistics
- Be able to retell and synthesize the essential points of the speech or story

- Be comfortable in your chair
- Most important, focus your attention on the speech

Active listening takes a great deal of practice and hard work, but its rewards are significant.

EGO DEFENSE MECHANISMS

Let's be frank. If you learn to swim, you are going to get wet. If you learn to ride a bicycle, you are going to skin a knee. If you learn to speak in public, you are going to receive some critical commentary from members of your speech study group.

Take this unavoidable fact and tuck it away in your mind. Once you have parked this safely in your psyche and know that you are going to take some verbal hits, you can then move forward with the rest of the people who take this conversational leap of faith.

Not knowing this universal truth can lead to some problems. Many speakers sometimes ignore valid, constructive comments just to protect their pride. You must be careful not to overlook helpful critiques just because they are not what you want to hear. These are some of the classic speaker's ego defense mechanisms to dodge the reality of the situation and how they usually sound:

- *Projection.* Put the blame elsewhere. "Oh, I did badly because the principal is ridiculous."
- *Escape.* Simply deny reality. "Hey, my speech was great; if you don't like it, it's your problem."
- *Rationalization.* Try to explain away a poor speech. "Oh, I didn't like the audience anyway."
- *Back Step.* Unfortunately, this one is very popular among some speakers; it means lowering one's maturity level to respond to a negative critique. "Oh well, you're wrong, pal, my speech was fine. You want to make something of it?"
- *Repression.* The brain accidentally forgetting a negative critique. "Oh, I forgot your comment somehow; silly me."

3

Writing Your Speech

HELPING THE WRITER: WRITING YOUR SPEECH

Just as with literature, where you can make the argument that all books boil down to five or six basic plots, so you can claim that in all the millions of kinds of speeches, they all reduce to six basic types, which can then be presented in any number of different ways. The basic types you will work with are

- *Argumentative, persuasive, or sales*—trying to change or strengthen an audience's position on an issue
- *Narrative or entertaining*—illustrating issues by showing the passage of time or the development of a plot or a story
- *Descriptive, interpretive, or inflecting*—painting verbal pictures, attempting to appeal to the audience's five senses to help them grasp issues
- *Informative, training, or reporting*—the telling of facts
- *Discursive*—positively using audience participation
- *Prescriptive, lecturing, or how to*—giving information with a specific behavioral or conceptual goal in mind for the audience

If you keep in mind that every speech, no matter how complicated, is just one of these types, you can keep everything in perspective.

CREATING YOUR OBJECTIVES FOR THE SPEECH

As a rule, people do not do things without a reason. Sometimes these reasons are clear, and sometimes the reasons or motivations may have a **hidden agenda.** In any case, you still need a good reason to spend a good deal of your time and emotional energy preparing a speech to deliver before a live audience.

Another way to think about reasons is to consider what teachers would call objectives. Objectives are what teachers want the students to learn, how they will learn it and in what order, what materials they need, and how you will assess if the students have learned the material content and you have fulfilled your objective. You need to be thinking like the educator you are for this activity to be helpful for you.

First, you should have a good idea who will be sitting in your audience. Next, you need to be able to decide what you want to accomplish with your speech. What do you want the listeners to do after you speak? Should they just be informed about a topic? Should they go out and buy something? Do you want them to write a member of the board? How should they feel after your speech? Happy, sad, excited, depressed, frightened? Once you have these decisions firmly in your mind, you can make more informed choices about the words and phrases you use to construct your speech.

THE HANDS-ON ORGANIZER

For some teachers, principals, and school administrators, organizing their thoughts for a speech topic is a most perplexing and sometimes even kind of a scary chore. From the volumes of the research published during the recent decade devoted to the functioning of the brain, is it possible that speakers can use some of this information to draft a hands-on speech without going back to graduate school for an advanced degree in neuroscience? The answer is, of course, *yes*. As a practical example of this, here is a model that you can employ to find order in your brainstormed chaos by actively processing work in both your visual and kinesthetic realms. In other words, it's okay to get your hands a little messy when making a speech.

In every speaking situation—from seventh-grade art class to the board of education—a good speech can help you become a better communicator in the new millennium.

A good speech gives you the confidence to do what you need to do when you stand up on your own two feet. Knowing that you have a well-prepared speech that makes sense to you will go a long way toward helping you make an effective presentation before a live audience. Remember, as Louis Pasteur said in 1854, "Chance favors the prepared mind." Give yourself the best chance possible for success.

For illustrative purposes, use the informative, training, or reporting speech described above as a model for the hands-on speech organizer. This could then be applied to the informational presentations section in Chapter 15. As you will see later, however, this technique will work just as well for any other type of speech.

Arriving at a Speech-Focusing Statement

The order and logical development of your speech is critical to its success. You should first consider the **speech-focusing statement,** or what English teachers call the *thesis statement,* in the hopes that it may provide the clues for the rest of the speech. The speech-focusing statement is your main idea of a speech that tells the listeners the purpose behind the piece. It needs to be a clearly written and interesting road map for the listeners to be able to comprehend where the speech is heading. The speech-focusing statement is the backbone of a speech: the main point, the central idea. Unfortunately, what you usually hear is a simple restatement of the topic for the speech. If you were teaching English 10 and the topic you assigned was, "Discuss the relationship between Hamlet and Ophelia," most students' introductions would include a sentence that begins, "Hamlet and Ophelia knew each other..."

Writing a speech-focusing statement, on the other hand, forces you to make an assertion; you have to take a stand on the topic. By choosing narrow details about a wide-open topic, speakers make conscious decisions about what they like, feel, and support. There are thousands of facts about each topic; why did the speaker choose these details? In composing a speech-focusing statement, you as the speaker are fashioning an opinion merely by stating the facts.

Advanced Webbing Techniques

With this charge in mind, here is a five-step procedure that appeals to all educators. It may look a bit daunting at first, but once you try it, you will be amazed how quickly you can comprehend the concepts behind these webbing techniques.

Put aside for the moment that you need to write a speech for the chamber of commerce. Instead, try to remember what it was like sitting in that 10th-grade English class. Consider the steps you would take in writing your essay.

Step One: Talk Before You Think

First, take a look at a routine speech undertaking, such as the aforementioned, "Discuss the relationship between Hamlet and Ophelia." If there is no research work involved, skip down a paragraph.

If there is research involved, it is at this early point that you should do your digging. Visit the library, interview your colleagues, visit a parents' meeting, make a few calls, surf the Internet, or follow whatever procedure you like for researching as much data as possible on the topic. Each researched fraction of data should be written down on a separate piece of paper or on a separate, small index card. Finally, randomly spread these **idea cards** or papers across a table.

If the topic did not involve any formal research, such as a personal reflective speech, and you had to invent or imagine the various details about a topic, then your first step is brainstorming.

A good technique to use for brainstorming is to find a quiet room somewhere, turn on a tape recorder, and say everything that pops into your mind when reflecting on the topic. Or, talk before you think. If no tape recorder is available, write each idea as quickly as possible. Try to brainstorm nouns, verbs, descriptions, and questions about the topic. Some types of questions are, What do you want to know about the topic? How can you use the topic or your knowledge about the topic? How does the topic relate to other things you know about? How do you feel about the topic? Once the brainstorming is finished, transcribe the tape by writing each idea on a separate piece of paper or on a separate, small index card (see Table 3.1).

Another enormously popular approach is to write the ideas on one single sheet of paper and then to use your fingers to rip the document so each idea is on its own shred of paper. If nobody is looking, you might try sitting on the floor as you do this to complete the effect. Either way, randomly spread these idea papers or cards across a table.

Step Two: Making Sense
Is in the Eye and Mind of the Beholder

Once you have spread the cards or papers—either researched or brainstormed—simply look at the cards or papers as a whole for several minutes. Do you see any patterns? Are some ideas very similar or very different? Do some of the ideas make better sense than the others? If an idea does not seem to fit with the others, throw it off the table and keep going until you have somewhere between 8 and 15 cards or papers left on the table. This begins the process of working with and reacting to visual and kinesthetic stimuli.

Table 3.1   Brainstorming Worksheet

Copy on this worksheet the ideas that pop into your head.

_____

_____

_____

_____

With the remaining cards or papers, begin moving them around the table to form an arrangement that makes sense to you. It does not matter what kind of sense it makes to anyone else, as long as it seems right to you. You are making mental interconnections, or categorizing the ideas at this point, as a metacognitive process in which you uncover contextual relationships that make sense to you and you alone.

Step Three: From Scraps to Maps

Copy the exact pattern of ideas precisely as it sits on the table during Step Two into a writing notebook, except now you should be drawing a circle around each idea and randomly labeling each circle as idea #1, idea #2, idea #3, and so forth.

Once copied, draw some lines between the ideas that seem related in any fashion or that made sense to you when you were thinking about the relationships among the ideas. One line should connect only two ideas. If there are two lines between two ideas, as a cleaner shortcut, you can draw a dashed line between the two ideas. You have now begun mapping your concepts of the topic.

Next, briefly label each line on the page to help jog your memories later; answer the questions, How does each idea on the line relate to the other? Is one idea a subset of the other? Does one cause the other to happen? Did one idea happen before the other? Does each of the ideas affect each other?

As an option at this point, you may want to put arrows at the ends of the lines.

A one-way arrow indicates that A is either a subset of B or, in other words, A is a member of the B group (e.g., Hamlet [A] is a member of the Danish royalty [B]); or that A causes B to happen; or that A happened before B. *Note:* you can have one line pointing one way and a second line pointing back to show that the two ideas affect each other—a dashed line between the two then represents this.

Now count the lines between the ideas to determine which idea has the most lines attached to it. Remember to count a dashed line as two lines. Call this idea with the most lines attached to it the *important idea*. If there is a tie, decide quickly off the top of your head which idea seems more important.

Next, list which remaining ideas are directly connected or not removed by more than one other idea to the important idea. From that list, rank order the ideas that have the most lines attached to them on the page from greatest to least. Then, make a short list of the top three from that list. In other words, of the ideas attached to the important idea or not off by more than one, which three have the most connections with the rest of the ideas on the page? Again, if there is a tie, decide quickly which ones seem more important. Now you will need to rank order the top three ideas on the short list. Of these three, which ones are directly connected to the important idea? Rank order these on top of the short list. Finally, of the directly connected ideas on the short list, decide which was drawn physically closest to the important idea. Use these criteria to make your final ranking by putting the closest idea on top of the short list. Write *item 1, item 2,* and *item 3* next to these ideas on your short list. Table 3.2 highlights the steps for sorting the ideas.

Step Four: Webbing Success

Next, prepare a new sheet of paper. In the middle of the paper, draw a three-inch-diameter circle. In the middle of the circle, copy the idea from the other page that had the most

Table 3.2   Shortcuts for Sorting Ideas

Description	Step Number	Notes
Count the lines between the ideas.	1	Count a dashed line as two lines.
If there is a tie, quickly decide which idea seems more important.	2	
Idea with the most lines attached to it becomes the "important" idea.	3	
List those remaining ideas directly connected (or not removed by more than one other idea) to the important idea.	4	
On this list, rank order the ideas that have the most lines attached to them—from greatest to least.	5	
Make a *short list* of the top three ideas from that list.	6	If there is a tie, quickly decide which idea seems more important.
Rank order the top three ideas on the *short list:*	7	
A. Which ones are directly connected to the important idea?		
B. Of the directly connected ideas on the *short list*, which one was drawn physically closest to the important idea?		

lines attached to it, the important idea. This term is now in the center of your web and is called the **hub.**

Draw three more circles around the center hub at 2 o'clock, 6 o'clock, and 10 o'clock, and draw temporary lines from these circles to the hub. Copy items 1, 2, and 3 from the short list into these circles. Next, draw the lines out from the items 1, 2, and 3 circles in the same way they appeared in your previous drawing, and copy your attached ideas from the previous page. In other words, attach the other ideas that were previously linked to items 1, 2, and 3. Finally, erase the original three temporary lines from the hub to items 1, 2, and 3.

You can refer to the Hub and Web Worksheet in Resource B for an illustration of this step.

Step Five: No-Fuss Speech-Focusing Statements

You will be amazed how remarkably simple this next step is. By duplicating the process speech-writing model discussed later in this chapter, you can now plug in the items from the web you made to create a preliminary speech-focusing statement, which could be positioned near the end of your speech's introduction: "This speech will [choose one: explore, explain, discuss, demonstrate, review, etc.] [name your hub] by examining [list item 1, item 2, and item 3]."

Please note this issue: Some educators prefer that the speech-focusing statement appears at the beginning of the introduction, which will work with this model as well. Even if you do not design your informative speech to follow this structure, you can still use the web as a focus for your thoughts and use the model as a backbone for your speech's development.

Once you have developed this preliminary speech-focusing statement, you can then develop an outline for the speech. The speech-focusing statement appears at the bottom (or top) of the introduction phase of the speech. Next, item 1 becomes the subject of the topic sentence for the first group of paragraphs; use the other items that are attached to it on the web as supporting information according to how the arrows indicate usage.

The process then repeats for item 2 and item 3 as you provide the subjects for the topic sentences and supporting issues for subsequent paragraphs using a typical process speech-writing model.

Process Speech-Writing Model

Here is a fill-in-the-blanks speech outline:

1. Introduction
    A. Catch listeners' attention (welcome).
    B. Begin to focus the issues.
    C. Speech-focusing statement:_____

    _____

    _____

2. Body Paragraph One
    Item 1: _____
        Strands from item 1: _____

        _____

3. Body Paragraph Two
    Item 2: _____
        Strands from item 2: _____

        _____

4. Body Paragraph Three
    Item 3: _____
        Strands from item 3: _____

        _____

5. Conclusion
    A. Restate speech-focusing statement: _____

    _____

    _____

    B. Move from specific to general issues.
    C. Explain to audience why it is or was important they heard this speech.

After you have your outline, you can begin filling in facts, details, quotes from parents, statistics, or whatever else you need to support the topic sentences of the paragraphs. The best way to begin this step is to use the other items on the web as modifiers to the main items.

As the first draft of the speech begins to take form, you will most likely realize that you need to change some of the wording of the speech-focusing statement, which is fine. In fact, you should find a more appropriate introduction than "This speech will" or "By examining." The true function of the preliminary speech-focusing statement is to provide direction during the early going of creating your speech; however, the order of items and the hub should be preserved. As the actual speech is developed in the process speech-writing model discussed earlier in this chapter, you will tinker with the speech-focusing statement until you have reached the final-draft form of the speech and the final or definitive speech-focusing statement that best addresses your audience's needs. The chamber of commerce will thank you.

Applications for Other Speech Types

Does this mean, then, that you can only use this technique when creating informative speeches? No, because the idea behind the procedure is to organize your thoughts to find your own connections, which works just as well with persuasive, entertaining, disciplinary, or other types of speeches.

For example, does this process work for writing a story for a story time at the local library? Yes, use the same steps up to the fill-in-the-outline section. Then, think of a new outline form. For example, the hub could be the main plot development in the rising action, with the three main ideas being significant plot points, setting, theme, or dialogue, depending on what you value in a story. If you are writing a poem, the hub could be your theme, and the three main ideas could be the tone, meaning, speaker, diction, or imagery, depending on what you value in a poem. If you are writing a science-based lab report speech for your science department, the hub could be the hypothesis, and the three main ideas could be three of these—procedure, equipment, variables, materials, safety precautions, observations, or results—depending on the nature of the lab. If you are writing a persuasive speech for your building, the hub could be the focal issue, and the three main ideas could then support your posture.

Different tasks call for different tools, however. When writing speeches, you can learn to appreciate writing more by adding some new tools to the shed. By appealing to your different learning styles and modalities, you can reach goals that before ended only in frustration and fussing, much as creating speeches did.

PROCESS SPEECH WRITING:
APPLICATIONS AND IDEAS FOR SPEECH WRITING

The key to writing a speech once you have your speech-focusing statement is to understand process speech writing. Much the same way math teachers send homework back for re-do's, you have to get accustomed to the idea that a perfect speech is not going to flow from your pen or word processor every time you sit down to write. It takes several rewrites before a speech can really meet your needs and the needs of the audience.

Part of functioning in a global community means understanding how to work within a team and appreciating how things that may seem different are actually connected. This understanding of connectedness in speech writing is critical to your growth as a speaker. In the same way, the ability of your audience to grasp your meaning is based on what they already know about a topic. Cognitive theories of understanding state that learning takes place only when the new learning is based on previous learning. The audience learning new material based on what they have previously mastered is much like a person climbing a ladder; you can climb to a new height only one rung at a time.

Creating the rest of your speech is very much like the connectedness exercises you performed to create your speech-focusing statement. Try to bring in as many supportive topics as possible to help your audience grasp meaning in your presentation.

Process speech writing is also like climbing that ladder. You constantly need to bring into the discussions the lessons that have come before and to show the connections among what is being learned. In business, the sales report takes on new meaning when the product is given relevancy in the listeners' minds by showing how it surpasses or replaces a well-known item.

The philosophy of speech writing can be summed up in one phrase: audience involvement. What is the best way to make sure that your audience is involved in your speech? Involve your speech study group as you are writing the speech. If you are not working within a speech study group, try to use some of your peers as colleague-editors before you create your final-speech draft.

Process speech writing should take place within your speech study group as the speech is being developed. Colleague consulting or conferencing is an important means of appraising the speech-writing process. A consultation is a great way to assess how the speech is developing. The key to success in the consultation lies in asking questions that help you focus your speech-writing plans. The following are examples:

- What is your speech-focusing statement?
- How did you arrive at the speech-focusing statement?
- Did you do any research?
- Are you following your web?
- What kind of audience do you expect?
- Are you writing a speech that makes sense to you?
- Are you writing a speech that will meet the audience's needs?
- Does your speech build on the audience's previous knowledge, or is it all brand-new?

As noted, once you have your first draft, you can begin the process of colleague-editing within your speech study group. You should work with your group members in reviewing and commenting on each other's work at several points. The normal flow of colleague-editing a speech is this:

1. Review of your outline or web by your boss (usually reserved for major works).

2. Colleague-editing by two or three peers. This is the small-group-editing phase. Take a full sheet of paper and

divide it with horizontal lines into four equal sections. On the top section put your name, the topic of your speech, and briefly state the speech-focusing statement. For sections two, three, and four, write at the top of the section:

Reader # ____'s Comments. Reviewed by _____.
Instruct the group:

> Feel free to offer whatever insights you feel might help me reach my best speech. You may want to consider major issues such as logical organization, focus of the speech-focusing statement, meaning of the speech, and other whole-speech topics. In general, although speeches and written works are very different, if a speech does not work well as a written document, it will not present itself well as a spoken passage. Your colleague review comments must be recorded on the review sheet (or attach another sheet if the comments are extensive). Also, please do not write on my original draft.

Paperclip this work sheet on top of the draft. Remember to number and date each draft. Keep all your drafts together, and attach them to a copy of your final speech for review later.

3. Boss consultation: You might want to meet with the boss for a brief consultation to review your progress.

4. Large-group review: You may volunteer to have sections (intros, conclusions, speech-focusing statements, etc.) of your drafts, from either the rough draft or a revised draft, put on transparencies for large-group discussions. This phase of the process is wonderful for the speech study group. You can learn more from each other's mistakes and successes than you can imagine. Becoming familiar with each other's styles and works can only strengthen your own speech writing.

5. Publishing and sharing: When all the work is finished, it is a good idea to make copies of your final draft and share them with the members of your speech study group. There is

something about seeing your words in print that really validates your efforts. You can also build up a pretty good library of speeches in your portfolio, which can help you down the line as models for creating new speeches.

DEVELOPING A RUBRIC FOR ASSESSING WRITTEN SPEECHES

So, how do you decide how well a speech is written? The best process is to develop a scoring **rubric** for your speeches. These are the criteria that you use for grading your speech-writing efforts. Once your speech study group has agreed on these standards, you can use these when you edit your peers' speeches in the future. In other words, you are going to decide what is important about your speech writing—what is good and what is not so good. Your speech study group can discuss what good really means. What does each good element look like?

What does excellent look like? What does basic look like? You can then create a list of observable traits that indicate what the element means. The group will take your assessment criteria and develop a 1-to-4 analytic scoring rubric with 4 points being the highest rating for each criterion and 1 point being the lowest (see Table 3.3).

For example, if your speech study group is writing an informative speech such as you would in Chapter 15, you might decide to look at the elements that would be important in your minds for assessing that kind of speech. You might decide on such criteria as "analysis of the topic," "Does the speech use proper reasoning?" "Is there enough proof to act as evidence that your speech works?" "Is there a clear opening, middle, and end to the speech?" "Does the speech instruct the listener what to do with the information?" and "Will the speech attract and hold the targeted audience's interest for the duration of the speech?" If these are your *assessment criteria*, you could summarize these points this way:

- *Analysis:* How well does the speech reflect an understanding of the topic?
- *Reasoning:* Is the speech believable, and does the audience have enough background to understand the new material?
- *Evidence:* Is there enough information given to prove your points?
- *Organization:* Does the speech flow from beginning to end?
- *Interest:* Will the speech be interesting to its audience?

For each rubric you create, you should follow this formula. First, decide what the objective for the speech will be in terms of how you want the audience to react. Continuing the work you did earlier in this section, try to fill in the blanks for the objective:

Speech Objective: This speech will (encourage, motivate, inform, etc.) my audience to (learn more, buy something for my department, do something, etc.).

Next, you decide on your evidence, or what proof you offer in the speech that it will meet the objectives. Again, fill in the blanks for your evidence:

Speech Evidence: The objective will be evident when the speech contains these elements (list the hoops, or criteria, through which the speech must jump here).

Finally, you have to build in an assessment piece. There are two parts to the assessment. First, what are the observable criteria that the speech must have to evidence that it is meeting its objective? Second, what is the rating scale (usually 1 through 4 works well) that you will use?

Once you decide on the scale, then you need some observable and easily understandable descriptions of what each point value means. What does a 4-point assessment really look like? What does a 1-point assessment look like?

(Text continues on page 36)

Table 3.3 Blank, Generic Speech Rubric

1	2	3	4	5	6
Rating Criteria	*Excellent Speech* 4 Points	*Very Good Speech* 3 Points	*Good Speech* 2 Points	*Basic Speech* 1 Point	**Score**
Criterion #1 The speaker will demonstrate/ present:	[*Note:* List exemplars— descriptions and observable traits in these boxes.]				
Criterion #2 The speaker will demonstrate/ present:					

(Continued)

Table 3.3 Continued

1	2	3	4	5	6
Criterion # 3 The speaker will demonstrate/present:					
Criterion # 4 The speaker will demonstrate/present:					
Criterion # 5 The speaker will demonstrate/present…					
			[*Note:* If total score is below an agreed-on result, consider further editing.]		**Total Score =**

Table 3.4 Fully Detailed Speech Rubric

1	2	3	4	5	6
Rating Criteria	*Excellent Speech* 4 Points	*Very Good Speech* 3 Points	*Good Speech* 2 Points	*Basic Speech* 1 Point	**Score**
Criterion #1 The speaker will demonstrate an understanding of the topic.	Speaker supports speech-focusing statement with strong arguments and facts.	Speaker is unclear; speech-focusing statement might reflect some facts and reasons.	Speaker is difficult to understand; speech-focusing statement does not reflect facts and reasons.	Speaker's information is not related to the speech-focusing statement or has no speech-focusing statement.	
Criterion #2 The speaker will present a believable speech.	Speaker presents enough background information and is believable.	Speaker presents some background information and is believable.	Speaker presents little background information and is somewhat believable.	Speaker presents no background information and is not believable.	
Criterion #3 The speaker will present enough information	Speaker supports arguments with outstanding facts, details, and sources.	Speaker presents strong support and details for arguments.	Speaker offers little support for arguments.	Speaker doesn't support arguments.	

(Continued)

Table 3.4 Continued

1	2	3	4	5	6
to prove her or his points.					
Criterion #4 The speaker will present a speech that flows from beginning to end.	Speaker's speech has a well-defined intro, body, and conclusion.	Speaker's speech has a fairly distinct intro, body, and conclusion.	Speaker's speech has an unclear intro, body, and conclusion.	Speaker's speech has no intro, body, or conclusion.	
Criterion #5 The speaker will present an interesting speech.	Speaker's speech is interesting and worthwhile.	Speaker's speech is still somewhat interesting.	Speaker's speech is boring or somewhat uncreative.	Speaker's speech is not at all creative or is hard to follow.	
					Total Score =

Your next step within the group is to agree on these rating exemplars, or more simply, what would a good speech look like for each criterion? For your purposes, what does a very good, or 4-point, analysis look like? Have these discussions within your group for each criterion so that you can create a document that everyone can use to find examples or descriptions of each criterion. For example, here are some illustrative descriptors for criterion number five:

Interest:

4 Points. The speech is
>   Interesting and worthwhile
>   Well-defined with clear central idea
>   Supported with large amounts of relevant and appealing details
3 Points. The speech is
>   Still somewhat interesting
>   Defined—point of speech somewhat easy to find but not as obvious as it might be
>   Supported with fair amount of general detail but might be repetitious
2 Points. The speech is
>   Boring or somewhat uncreative
>   Short on relevant detail
>   Extremely hard to decipher in terms of the point
1 Point. The speech is
>   Not at all creative, hard to follow
>   Without detail
>   Without an apparent point

Building the Rubric

Once you have your five or so hoops through which the speech must jump, you can then build an assessment rubric, or graphic chart, to help you evaluate everyone's speeches. Table 3.3 is a blank generic speech rubric that you can reproduce. On it, 4 is the highest rating for each criterion and 1 is the lowest.

In each square under the ratings, you should write in the descriptions and observable traits of each criterion at each point level, so that a colleague-editor can use this tool to rate how each criterion is progressing. The editor can then assign the point value in the score column that best resembles the progress for each criterion. Then, by adding the scores together and dividing by five, you have an overall numerical performance assessment that you can use for further editing of your speech. Table 3.4 is an example of a fully detailed speech rubric.

Finally, as a kind of closure on the whole process and to prepare yourself for the next speaking engagement, you might want to create an evaluation form for your audience, such as the Evaluation Form for Speaker and Program in Resource A, to help you make informed adjustments to your speeches in the future.

Speaking
Before
Student
Groups

4

Understanding and Managing Your Nervousness

Assemblies and Other Large Groups of Students

FIGHT OR FLIGHT

Standing before a group of students and delivering a speech can be one of the most intimidating experiences of your life. Your heart starts to race, the blood leaves your fingers and toes, your throat goes dry, you shake, and you really wonder why in the world you are doing this.

PSYCHOSOMATIC STRESS

Well, don't worry. This is quite normal. Your body is undergoing what is known as psychological or **psychosomatic stress.**

The bad news is that there really is not too much you can do about it. As you will discover later, the body is going to react that way no matter what you do. In fact, the process can be broken down into four distinct phases, which are typical of most stressful situations:

1. *Your assignment.* This is the stressor or cause of your anxiety. "You must address the high school next Tuesday."

2. *Conception and reaction.* You consciously react. "I'm afraid of speaking in front of people. Oh, man, I'm dead."

3. *The body reacts.* All sorts of natural yet nasty chemicals are dumped into the bloodstream (as discussed later in this chapter). "Oh, my stomach hurts."

4. *Result.* A nervous start to your presentation. "I, ah, would like to welcome you, and, uh . . ."

Once you understand your fears, you will be able to cope with your conception and reaction. You cannot avoid these speaking situations, but you must contain your attitude about them.

PHYSICAL REACTIONS TO SPEAKING

Your body has a complex reaction to speech making or any perceived stressor or danger. This reaction has been a function of humans for a very long time. Once you get ready to begin, your **hypothalamus** kicks in. Your hypothalamus is the basal section of your thalamus, which lies in the base of your brain and controls the autonomic nervous system. The hypothalamus activates two systems, the nervous system and the endocrine system.

The nervous system is the sympathetic division of the autonomic nervous system, which activates involuntary muscles and the medulla of the **adrenal glands,** which are located near your kidneys. The adrenal glands release a natural, powerful heart stimulant known as **adrenaline** (epinephrine) and its helper **noradrenaline** (norepinephrine) into the bloodstream.

Meanwhile, the endocrine system activates the anterior pituitary gland at the base of the brain to release the **adreno-corticotrophic hormone (ACTH).** ACTH stimulates the cortex of the adrenal glands and thyroid to produce **corticosteroids.**

What all this means is that when adrenaline, nor-adrenaline, and corticosteroids are let loose in your body, some rather nefarious things begin to happen to you. Your heart rate increases, your blood pressure increases, your oxygen level increases, the blood leaves your external body parts and your digestive system and rushes to the large muscles, and your brain activity changes. Your body and brain give you only two choices, run or fight. This is known as the **fight or flight** reaction. Living in a mature, politically correct society that would frown on your obliterating entire auditoriums full of children or jumping out of the window leaves you with few options except to deliver the speech.

Most sensible people—without the benefit of this book— would rather play around and make jokes when it comes time to speak rather than to admit the truth. You're scared, and now you know that you have a right to be.

SPEAKING TACTICS

Before you go up to speak, you may want to try a few speaking tactics. Take a few slow, deep breaths. Force yourself to yawn a few times. Let your body go limp. Nobody is sure why these work, but they do seem to ease the tension. Later, you will discover how to make your nervousness actually work in your favor.

For now, it is critical that you understand that the physiological reactions that occur when you are about to make a speech do not last, on average, for more than 90 seconds once you have started your presentation. This means that if you can live through the first minute or so of your presentation, all the defense systems of the body start to relax. Have you ever heard someone say, "Well, I was nervous when I got up there, but after a little while, I was fine." This happens because under normal circumstances, chemicals are no longer awash in your system after 90 seconds. The physiological reactions decline is a natural occurrence that you can rely on happening when you stand up to speak.

Armed with this knowledge, consciously accept the fact that you will be nervous going into your speech. You can also understand that if you can just get through the first minute, everything will be all right. How do you do this? *Practice the opening of your speech more than any other part so that you are almost on automatic pilot when you start.* Your opening will get the students on your side, and you will witness early signs of approval. When the chemistry dies down, you will be able to think more clearly and can make whatever speaking or reading adjustments you need to make.

SELF-FULFILLING PROPHECY

If this is your first time before a large student group, you need a reality check here; most people do poorly their first time speaking before a group. You should expect it. Simply doing this speech will give you the courage to go on.

What you must do is avoid a self-fulfilling prophecy here. After delivering a less-than-stellar performance on a speech, some people take that as a permanent indication of their ability as a speaker. A poor performance on this speech should not convince you that you are a total failure but rather that you are quite normal.

THE SHAKING VOICE AND VOCAL WARM-UPS

Athletes do not just walk out onto the field and start their games—they take special care to warm up before they play.

Teachers, principals, and school administrators must do the same thing; it is called the vocal warm-up. The vocal warm-up stretches the mouth out and gives the lungs 40% to 60% more available space to use for projection. It looks as if you are swallowing a watermelon when you are doing it, so you might want to do this warm-up in private at least one-half hour before you speak.

The first thing you do is take a good, deep breath, and then slur through your vowels one at a time in a constant, droning voice, stretching your lips and mouth to exaggerate the sounds. Keep running through the vowels, making the kinds of sounds that you would when the doctor is checking your tonsils, until you run out of air. Then take another deep breath and do it all again. Make up some weird sounds and change your volume as you do this exercise three times. If you have to do this in public before the students, just put your hand in front of your mouth and pretend that you are yawning. This may make as much sense to you as wearing a tuxedo to a beach party, but try it—the experts swear by it.

VOCAL RANGES

While making a speech can make you feel out of control, in fact, there are four elements to your vocal range that you can control:

■ **The pitch.** Do not squeak too high or boom too low.

■ **The volume.** Project from your diaphragm, not from your throat. Practice this by putting your hand on your chest, speaking at different volumes, and trying to feel the vibrations. In singing, you would have someone concentrate on the diaphragm area and how it expands to fill the lungs with air and then pushes the air out.

■ **The pace.** Try to stay between 130 and 160 words per minute.

■ **The quality.** Try to keep your voice rich, and avoid slips in diction and enunciation.

All this is fine, but what do you do about those butterflies caged in your esophagus? Can you control your nerves? Sorry, no.

MAKING NERVOUSNESS WORK FOR YOU

Face it, you cannot control your nerves, and you know why—the adrenaline is pumping through your body. So why try to control your nerves—contain them and use them to your advantage. Nervousness means adrenaline, and adrenaline means energy—use the energy. Do not try to fight it, go with it. Have your speech so well prepared that you are like a rocket ready to blast off. If you are prepared, then you are ready. If you are not prepared, then and only then do you have a good reason to worry. You know what to do and how to do it—go for it. The students will appreciate your effort.

LAST-MINUTE NERVES AND SOLUTIONS

Sometimes, no matter how psyched up you are, some things still seem to be happening to your body. Here is a list of the last-minute nervousness problems you may have and how to deal with them.

1. *Tongue-tied*—you start tripping over simple words. Of course, your tongue is not really tied, nor is it taking a holiday. The remedy to this problem is very simple—just slow down.

2. *Sweating*—you cannot dry off your hands or face. The remedy is to look over the group's heads or pick out a few friendly faces to focus on. If this does not work, just imagine that your boss somewhere in the audience is stark naked except for a few fig leaves. This always seems to work for some strange reason.

3. *Muscle cramps*—all of a sudden your muscles freeze. Remedy: They are not really frozen; they are just lacking blood pressure. Gesture and take a few steps, and the cramps will disappear.

4. *World War III in your stomach*—the classic butterfly syndrome. Remedy: Just remember why it is happening, and then suppress thinking about it. Once you get into your speech, you will forget about your stomach as your physiology changes.

5. *Shaking*—your hands are shaking like the proverbial leaf. Remedy: You cannot stop them from shaking at that moment, so either grab the sides of the podium or put your hands behind your back. Again, do not worry, it will stop.

5

Involving Your Audience

Team or Grade-Level Student Meetings

AUDIENCE PARTICIPATION TACTICS

It is fair to say that different kinds of speeches call for different levels of student participation and interaction. When interacting with students in a smaller forum, you will be asking them to participate. However, asking an audience to participate is a very risky venture. When you are delivering a routine public speech, most people are content to sit back and listen. When you call for participation, you are involving them physically and actively in the process of your speech. When you give up this kind of control, you need to be able to pull back the reins when the time comes. Stand-up comedians rely on audience participation to provide fodder for their act. Nevertheless, you should know that while stand-up comedians appear to be reacting spontaneously to what the people say, they have spent many long hours preparing what-if scenarios so that they have a quick response no matter what anyone says or does.

In general, when discussing an issue or delivering information, you call for student participation as a strategy for getting them on your side, making them think that you are one of them and that you are all together on a single issue, or are one of the gang. In terms of presentation, this can take on three levels of difficulty.

■ The easy level—ask the students routine questions before you get to the introduction of your speech. For example, you can ask who has the same first name as you or the same birth date or where the people are from, which is more of a warm-up than a real interaction.

■ The moderate level—ask volunteers to help with a demonstration or ask questions to solicit answers.

■ The difficult level—invite comments or arguments on issues that you bring to the floor. This can take on a press conference feel, so you should avoid it unless you are ready for a conflict.

Another form of audience participation is your ability to watch your student audience and adjust your presentation accordingly to the nonverbal cues you receive from them. This will be covered in Chapter 8.

DEALING WITH DISTRACTIONS

You should become well acquainted with the notes you are about to deliver. After all, you are the world's leading expert on your notes, so go for it! You should be so familiar with your plans that if a distraction occurs, such as someone entering the room or someone laughing, you can deal with it. The mistake that some teachers, principals, and school administrators make is that they try to ignore the distraction. Well, you cannot. You know it is there and so does everyone else, so you might as well acknowledge its existence. You should stay with your speech yet deal with the distraction. Just nod to the person who walked in on your speaking, point to a desk, and keep right on going. The key to coping with distractions is knowing your notes well enough that you can take the time to think about dealing with an unexpected variable.

6

Discovering What Is Really Important at Your School

Discipline Meetings

VALUE STRUCTURES

Discipline meetings are held for a number of reasons: to create new rules for your school, to decide on consequences for violating school rules, and, in some cases, to determine if a member of the school community has violated the school's trust by breaking some rules.

In any case, discussions such as these involve your school's values in making decisions, which sounds fine, but how do you as a leader in these situations explain what values are for your students, and when, as the adult, should you know when to step in and take control of the discussions?

Simply put in this context, *values are what you use to make decisions.* They are based on your background and appreciation of certain topics and beliefs. As an example, typical values in society might look and sound like this at a political rally:

- Life and basic survival needs
- Liberty and freedom
- Personal growth
- Creature comforts
- For country
- Social gain
- Survival

What are the important values in your school? Honesty? Respect? Privacy? Excellence?

Every school purports to embody all of these and other values. Your job is to try to discover what is real. The students know what's important in their community. You just have to help them articulate it. Having everyone agree on what's genuine is critical when determining issues surrounding discipline because often so much is at stake. The decisions you make about your school's discipline go a very long way in defining who you are as a school.

DECISION-MAKING TECHNIQUES

You will need to lead a discussion to determine your school's core values before you can start making any decisions about discipline. Why? Because the disciplinary decisions you make are based on what you think is important and what you value as a school. While almost every school has a mission statement or statement of philosophy, you still need to define it operationally for everyone to use. Unfortunately, in this world, there is no absolute judge who can decree whether someone is truly good or bad, or right or wrong. Therefore, you rely on your own background and sense of what is appropriate to help you along the path of decision making.

You make decisions every day. Some are simple, some are very difficult. It is estimated that the average person in one day makes around 200 action decisions. These are decisions that effect something or affect someone. In general, the greater the impact of the decision, the more difficult it becomes to make. You can begin to see this as you start with an examination of what you and your students value. To help shape this discussion, you might try this exercise to help the students focus their thoughts.

Exercise: Your Values Are

Have everyone in the meeting line up along a wall or in one of two corners to physically represent where they stand in relation to the following value statements. In other words, if you completely agree with a statement, go to this corner. If you completely disagree, stand in this corner. If you are in the middle, stand next to the wall between the two corners. Line up responding in order of agreement or disagreement to these ascending, value-based statements:

- Okay to be angry
- Okay to yell at a person
- Okay to lie
- Okay to break a rule
- Okay to hurt another person
- Okay to use illegal substances in school
- Okay to (fill in with the issues you are discussing)

Discuss among yourselves your stand on the issues. The important thing here is to ask the students why they stood where they did. The why often reveals the students' values and beliefs, which you can use later to help them reach decisions.

With how many of these questions did you find yourself saying things like, "I agree, except when . . ." Are your school's values absolute? When you start to chip away at a value, does it really become a slippery slope? Use these answers to help formulate where everyone stands on what's important in your school.

Decision-Making Models

Once you have established where everyone stands on your school's values, you can then use one of the following models to help the students reach some decisions about disciplinary issues.

Consensus

The best of all decisions arises from consensus, or the win-win approach. Here, everyone who has a stake in an issue joins together to examine the goods and bads of that issue and then reach a decision that every person can live with and support. It is the best decision since everyone supports it, but consensus decisions usually take a long time to happen. The essential phrase you hear in consensus building is, "While this may not be everything you wanted, can you live with and actively support what we have here?"

Approach–Avoidance Decision Making

For the sake of discussion, you can say *approach* means you want to do something good or fun, like seeing a movie. *Avoidance* means you do not want to do something you do not like, such as making your bed. There are three possible combinations:

Approach–avoid is an easy decision: skip the bed making and hit the Cineplex.

Avoid–avoid is more difficult; most people feel it is like choosing between two tribulations.

Approach–approach is actually the most difficult choice you have to make.

You can use approach and avoidance as labels when you are discussing multiple issues simultaneously.

Utilitarianism

■ Jeremy Bentham, a writer back in the 18th century, along with John Stuart Mill, talked about utilitarianism. They wrote the law of utility: The question is, What represents the most good for the greatest number of people? Do you agree? For example, the school might be examining a rule for the sake of the school's sense of security that might seem unfair to some students (e.g., jackets should not be worn in school).

Occam's Razor

■ William of Occam, an English monk who lived from 1285–1349, is credited with founding the law of parsimony, also known as Occam's Razor. This states that it is vain to do with more what can be done with less. This means that given two or more conflicting explanations, you should choose the one that is the most simple. On the other hand, if something happens that you cannot account for, you should always try to explain it first in terms of what is known. Rules that are simple are usually the best.

ADULT SPEAKING QUALITIES

Sometimes in a disciplinary meeting, despite everything that has been said up to this point, as the adult leader, you simply have to have the final word and tell everyone *the way it's going to be*. When you reach this decision, your public-speaking skills are really going to come in handy.

If you are trying to convince the students that something is important, always try to appeal to their primary (biological and psychological) and secondary (social) needs. In other words, an issue such as safety might outweigh an issue such as fun. Pulling rank is all right if the students see that it is necessary for the success of the meeting.

To help in this area, below are five suggestions for capturing the empathy and assents of your listeners.

- Catch the students' attention through a needs assessment. Why are they even at this meeting?
- Hold the students' attention via the dynamics of your presentation. Remind them what is at stake.
- Convince the students with your logic. Discipline issues are usually emotionally charged; try to keep the discussion more cerebral rather than visceral.
- Persuade the students with your motivating material. Do your homework beforehand.
- Elicit action from the students to opt for your position. After all, you are the teacher.

Affective Skills

Finally, when telling everyone the way it's going to be, it is important not to look bossy, even though, in fact, maybe you are. So as not to obviously appear that way, these issues are always important to keep in mind:

- Being sincere
- Being tactful
- Believing in what you are saying
- Exercising good taste in your statements

With these, the students should appreciate why you are taking the lead, and your message will be heard loud and clear.

7

Just
Showing Off

Talent Shows

Tone and Figurative Language

The assumption here is that you have decided to skip the juggling act this year and have decided to entertain the students by telling a funny story or with some other kind of entertaining speech. In order to entertain a group of students, you must have a fundamental understanding of the basics of tonal devices and figurative language. **Tone** is the sound property of your speech, and it includes the lyricism, rhythm and rhyme, musical considerations, and the oral figurative language. Figurative language is the use of words that represent other meanings. The basic elements of figurative language and tone are as follows:

1. Understatement is used to underscore an important idea with an ironic twist. Understatement extenuates the obvious and highlights the insignificant elements of a topic (e.g., "Churchill was a good golfer.").

2. Allusion hints at a topic but never comes right out and says what it really is. It would be like a child suggesting, "The hot dogs at Fred's Grill are yummy," but never saying that he actually wanted to eat there. Listeners are often left to draw their own inference.

3. Hyperbole is the opposite of understatement. Hyperbole blows everything out of proportion: It turns a common cold into fatal emphysema; it turns a cricket's chirp into a cacophony; it transforms puppy love into Romeo and Juliet. Hyperbole is overstatement.

4. Juxtaposition places opposite ideas side by side to create a new truth, much like a paradox or oxymoron. Some examples would be: "The soldier died to preserve life," "Hand me the diet ice cream," "This is almost exactly what I need," or "Now, then, I am driving to the sanitary landfill."

5. Metaphor and **simile** are the two primary forms of comparison in the English language. A metaphor is an implied comparison not using *like* or *as*. It is a figure of speech denoting an object or an idea. An example would be defining a camel as a *desert boat*. A camel is not a boat, but it acts like one in the desert. A simile is an implied comparison using *like* or *as*. "I'm as hungry as a bear." A simile does not imply that you are a bear the way a metaphor would; it merely notes a common trait.

6. Personification occurs if you give human characteristics to nonhumans. When the wind whispers and groans, or when a tree dances in a breeze, or a car sighs relief, you have personification.

7. Irony arises when something happens that is the opposite of what you expect. Usually irony involves a twist of fate or having a plot backfire:

The villain crept up behind the young hero with an evil looking, twisted knife in his wicked clutches. As he grew near, he raised the dreadful knife above his head as he prepared to strike. Unfortunately for the villain, he did not notice the stool on the floor. So, as he lunged toward the hero, the scoundrel tripped over the stool and drove the knife deep into his own nasty heart.

8. Sound devices are the musical variations you can make in your speech. The basic four are:

A. *Alliteration*—the repetition of initial sounds in words next to each other (e.g., big boys buy bread in baskets)

B. *Onomatopoeia*—making words from sounds (e.g., tick-tock, clang, pow)

C. *Assonance*—the repetition of vowel sounds in words next to each other (e.g., "the rare and radiant maiden")

D. *Consonance*—the repetition of consonant sounds in words next to each other—particularly at the end of stressed syllables (e.g., kill, sell)

9. Poetry writing tends to go better if you know these basic elements before you take a pen in hand:

- *Meaning and Value.* Content as judged by listener
- *Speaker of Poem.* Speaker/narrator (The narrator is not the author, and the speaker is not the poet. You as the presenter do not have to be the speaker in this case.)
- *Subject.* Literally, what the poem is about
- *Narrative or Epic Poem* (e.g., the *Odyssey* or *Paradise Lost*). Tells a poetic story of great people doing great things, which is always a popular choice
- *Lyrical Poetry.* A poem that can be sung—can and maybe should be a song
- *Tone of Voice.* Speaker's (not yours) attitude toward the subject of the poem
- *Gender.* Masculine (final syllable) and feminine (not final syllable) rhymes
- *Diction.* The words you choose to put in your poem

- *Imagery.* Triggers memories through listeners' senses and emotions
- *Poetry Allusions.* References in a poem to something or someone great or famous
- *Syntax.* The order of the words you choose to put in your poem
- *Theme.* Human motifs that contribute to the meaning (love, hate, jealousy, other emotions)

Now that you have seen the various elements of tone and figurative language, you have to decide what type of speech or act to write. There are really only two rules to keep in mind for an entertaining act:

- If you decide to poke fun at someone, poke fun at yourself first.
- Whatever you decide to do, keep in mind that an entertaining speech should sound good—remember your elements of tone.

Ideas for Topics for Your Speech

- **Satire**—a new spoken work that mocks human weaknesses
- **Parody**—a humorous imitation of a person, song, or book
- A humorous story
- A song
- A funny story
- A poem
- A stand-up comedy routine
- A retelling of classic stories with bizarre endings

DEALING WITH LAUGHTER

Wit is the ability to make humorous remarks; and wisdom is the experience you need in life to have the background and credibility to make the humor work. For example, a teenager can tell a perfectly delightful story about two old retired gentlemen playing chess. To his peers, it may strike them as funny, since they have no real frame of reference to judge the authenticity of the humor. To a room full of octogenarians, it would not seem as clever. Remember—you are an adult trying to entertain a room full of students, so keep their needs in mind.

If by some miracle the students do begin to laugh, remember the two policies for dealing with laughter:

1. Wait until the laughter starts to diminish before you give your next line. If you keep talking while the audience is laughing, you will teach them not to laugh because they will miss something. Just stay frozen in place until the time is right to continue.

2. Never laugh at your own jokes—the group will laugh at you, not with you. The best way to get the laughs out of your system is to tell the joke to a few people before your speech. It will be old news when you spring it on the group.

Try to use expressive language—words that will appeal to both the ear and the brain—and keep a logical order to your speech. There is nothing quite as embarrassing as telling a joke and giving the punch line too soon.

You Can't Please Everybody

Realize before you begin that you will not be able to entertain every member of the audience. This is what makes the human race so diverse. If everybody liked the same thing, there would be no variety. So do not be afraid to try something totally ridiculous; not everyone will like it, but, on the other hand, some will.

Your Body Language Speaks Volumes

Classroom (The Students Are Watching Your Every Move)

NONVERBAL COMMUNICATION

Many teachers assume that the only way they communicate to their students is through the words they say. Nothing could be further from the truth. Students are experts at spotting incongruities between what teachers say and what they mean.

Approximately a third of the message your students receive comes from your words, and the other two thirds come from nonverbal cues. When the verbal and nonverbal signals are contrasting (e.g., your voice sounds excited, but your body language and your eyes seem bored), the students will attend more to your body than your voice. They will see that you are bored and not pay attention to your verbal message. This is also why you need to pay attention to your dress, your nervous habits, your attitude about your topic, and your hand movements.

Knowing this, you should consider how you might communicate to your class without using words. Try asking yourself, How would a mime teach this lesson? There are some important aspects of communication that take place when you are not speaking, yet still communicating.

PROXEMICS

Pretend for a moment that you are going to teach a class without speaking. If this were truly a mimed lesson, all of the elements of body language (which is not a real language but is still a form of communication) would come into play: Your face, hands, feet, posture, and movement are all critical elements. **Proxemics,** the cultural understanding of the physical space between your body and things around it, is also very important.

MIMED SPEECH FACTORS

Consider some key factors to mimed communication:

■ The *head* is the most important factor in a mimed speech. It begins every movement and contains the brain. Your head can tilt and rotate and make facial expressions.

■ The *eyes* are said to be the gateways to the mind. They control the focus of attention and can act independently of the rest of the head. They can act in harmony with the rest of your body or act in ironic contrast. The eyes create the illusion of speaking or reacting to a speech or event.

■ The *mouth* cannot move to make words—that would be cheating. Nevertheless, it can show pleasure or displeasure, and it can taste, and it can form an O to show surprise.

■ The *ears*—you can turn your head to indicate hearing a sound.

■ The *torso*—you can't do too much with your trunk—there's not a lot to be expressive with; however, a certain posture can depict an emotion (a slump is unhappy, etc.).

■ The *hands* are very expressive. Control of your hands reflects your character.

■ *Legs* are the framework for your body. They show action and motion.

CLASSIC MIMED MOVEMENTS

A list of traditional mimed movements:

■ Move forward to agree or to comfort.
■ Move backward to display shock or surprise.
■ Hunch your shoulders to show sadness.
■ A quick turn indicates new "sentences" or that you have had an idea.

The following movements also have special meanings when teaching. These are the classic body-language movements (note that they are often used unconsciously):

■ Moving feet show nervousness.
■ Hands folded in front of your body show that you are not prepared and are worried.
■ Arms crossed across your chest is a defensive posture, as if to say, "Keep away."

- Hands behind your back or at your sides show confidence.
- Hands in your pockets suggest absent-mindedness.

Classic Body Language Movements

Sometimes you will not have the best lesson plan in the world, or your voice might be a little weak on a given day. It is good to know at times like these, if you understand body language, that your physical appearance will not give your secret away.

Speaking Before Parent Groups

9

Scheduled
Parent
Meetings

Parent-Teacher Conferences

BACK-TO-SCHOOL NIGHT MEETINGS

Nothing gets typical teachers' hearts racing faster than the thought of conducting small meetings with the parents of their darling students. These kinds of meetings traditionally take on one of two forms. The first is a brief presentation that you give for the parents of each of your classes, usually during a back-to-school kind of event. The second form is the face-to-face meeting where you chat with parents individually or as couples.

Under normal circumstances, the back-to-school presentations should be about your curriculum, your expectations and standards, and your homework and test policies—not about any individual students. You should always have descriptive handouts prepared ahead of time that you distribute at the start of the 10-minute meeting. Normally, you would never give out printed materials at the beginning of a presentation because some of the people would read the literature and ignore what you have to say. However, in this case, parents appreciate having something in their hands that they can focus on if they choose to do so. Remember, if this meeting is uncomfortable for you, it is just as uncomfortable for some of your parents. Not everyone had a memorable experience in school, and returning to the classroom sometimes can be a difficult experience. So giving them something to read might help make it a little more tolerable.

You might want to start the "class" by telling the parents an amusing anecdote from something that happened with that group's children during the year (no names, please). Never start with the meat of your presentation, because there will always be latecomers. Next, try to review the highlights of the handout without reading any parts of it verbatim. Be sure to have all your materials and textbooks available to use as visuals during your presentation. You could end the meeting with a brief question-and-answer session; however, make it clear first that you are prepared to talk only about curriculum. If someone asks a question that you are not prepared to answer, or a question about an individual student, always have a legal pad by your side and invite parents with questions to write down their names and phone numbers so you can make contact at a later (and more appropriate) time.

FACE-TO-FACE PARENT MEETINGS

The face-to-face meeting is a little more challenging for some teachers, principals, and school administrators; however, if you keep in mind some simple fundamentals, you will be fine. Be sure to have some refreshments in your room or nearby, and be sure to offer them to your parents before you begin the business part of the conversation. Also, be sure to thank them for taking the time to come and meet with you—they are making a sacrifice being there just as much as you are.

The most important thing to keep in mind when talking directly with parents is that in almost every instance, they are truly interested in their child's success and happiness, and they view you as an important person who can help them along the way.

When discussing a student's progress, keep these fundamentals in mind:

1. Stick to the facts. Discuss grades, tests, quizzes, papers, and any other assessment measures that you use. In discussing the facts, try to stay away from your interpretation of the facts or offering your opinions. Terms such as "I think" or "I feel" should be avoided.

2. Don't project how a student will do in your course. Stick to the here and now, and don't offer comments such as, "Oh, I am sure that Johnny will do fine if he studies some more." If he studies some more and his grade is not fine, guess whom the parents are going to hold responsible.

3. Always discuss how students perform relative only to themselves, not to the other children in the class.

4. Prepare notes on each student well ahead of time so that you do not appear to scramble when a question is asked.

5. Have an agenda for each parent and stick to it. Be polite and answer the parents' questions, but if something comes up that you are not ready or able to discuss, take their phone number and promise to call them the next day.

Keep the conversation focused on the student's performance—not on you as the teacher, or the parents, or anyone else. If a meeting ever takes a turn that seems uncomfortable for you, especially if a parent starts asking about your training or background in a fashion that is different from just being polite, do not hesitate to end the conversation and let the parent know that you would prefer to have an administrator with you before continuing.

10

Working With Parents on More Difficult Issues

Speaking Before Meetings to Address Parental Concerns

LEADING A COMMUNITY FORUM

On occasion, you might be asked to chair a community forum or a meeting where parents can gather to discuss their concerns. It is critical to the success of the meeting that, as the chair of the meeting, you know all the issues before the meeting. To accomplish this end, meet with a spokesperson for the parents and agree on each of the issues beforehand.

Going into an open-forum meeting, where concerns are collected from the floor, is a very challenging task for any person at any level of education, especially if you are expected to respond. The only common version of this open-forum approach is the open microphone or community forum at board of education meetings. Even here, the board members listen to the comments and are not expected to respond.

However, if you plan to answer questions, instead of just recognizing raised hands, try having anyone with a question write the question on a card before the meeting. Be sure to ask the people to sign their names and put down a phone number. Have a friend collect all of the cards during the meeting, and then sort them according to your topics for the night, and then by those you are capable of handling. Those questions that were off-topic or that you were not ready to handle publicly can be addressed in private with a phone call the next day.

Leading a meeting such as this can present some special challenges. Therefore if you are chairing a meeting to address parental concerns, after meeting with the parent representative and agreeing on the issues, be sure to follow this checklist for success:

1. Make sure your meeting is agenda driven. In other words, create an agenda and stick to it.

2. Do not deviate from your agenda. If people have new issues, thank them for their concern and ask them to meet with you privately for discussion, or say you will add the issue to a future agenda.

3. Keep control of the meeting. If it seems impossible to continue the meeting, it is usually better to thank everyone for coming and end the assembly rather than to turn over control of the agenda or the topics for discussion.

4. Remember, curriculum is not a neutral topic; people get excited about what their children are learning.

5. Do not allow surprise topics to be introduced at meetings.

DEALING WITH CONFLICT

One thing you should be ready for is conflict if certain concerns are involved. To meet this challenge, you should make use of the following tips:

- At the very beginning of the meeting, ask the audience to keep open minds and to postpone judgment until the end.
- Divorce yourself from the topics; in other words, do not become the authority figure—let your logic and evidence speak for themselves.
- Try to remain as empirical as possible—choose your evidence judiciously.

Remind your audience that facts do not lie. If memory serves, Aristotle, in his famous *Discourse on Rhetoric*, noted four major steps in winning an argument in the eyes of an audience (the art of **rhetoric**): Establish your arguments and attack the opponent's position; promote your strong arguments and minimize your weak claims; remind your audience what you are trying to prove several times during a speech; and put emotion into your presentation.

COMMUNICATION MYTHS

Here are some basic facts about communication you might want to review before the meeting to help you prepare. Communication is the process of giving and receiving information. Effective communication skills must be learned through experience and reflection; they are not with you at birth.

You can learn to communicate better in meetings if you can overcome these five typical myths about communication:

- The message sent is the message received. Wrong. People do not always interpret your words in the spirit in which they were sent.

■ You can stop communicating any time you want. Wrong. You cannot not communicate. Every move you make is a form of communication.

■ Facts are facts. Wrong. Some facts may seem valid enough to you because of your frame of reference. To an older person, the fact that "teenagers today are all irresponsible" may seem valid enough. Be sure to separate hard facts from soft-opinion facts. In addition, for what it is worth, in most cases, people's perceptions of someone or something are more real for them than the actual reality of the situation.

■ Only the words are important. Wrong. Just as a radio signal is transmitted by a carrier wave, our words are transmitted by a human voice. Sometimes humans have hidden agendas, or ulterior motives, behind their words in a meeting.

■ Reality is reality. Wrong. Reality all depends on your point of view. The best way to confirm a reality is to communicate information. For example, "an ounce of gold is valuable" seems realistic enough as a proposition. However, to a person dying of thirst in the desert, an ounce of gold is worthless. Now, if that person in the desert could find a desert telephone and call a desert gold dealer, then all the water desired would be made available. The truth of a given reality is best ensured through the listener's **reflection** of the message. In a conversation, this is accomplished by saying something like, "I think I heard you say . . ." and allowing the other person to confirm the interpretation or amend the thought.

11

Presenting a Persuasive Line of Reasoning

Speaking Before Budget Meetings

ELEMENTARY PERSUASION TECHNIQUES

Let's first set the stage for this kind of speech. You are asking people to spend more money for something that they cannot see, hold, smell, or taste. Improving the quality of education in some schools can be a very difficult sell. However, if you rely on your natural abilities, you can often be very successful.

Why? Because you are a natural persuader. You have done it all your life. Every time you enter a conversation, you engage in elementary persuasion techniques. It is true: Any time you make a statement of fact, you are asserting its validity and assuming that your listener agrees.

This budget speech goes further than a normal conversational assertion: Now you have to assume that not everyone will agree with you from the start, and it is your job to make them see things your way. The goal of this speech is to change someone's mind or way of thinking about your proposal. Your message is, of course, very important in this speech, but your voice and body language are even more important.

When you are trying to convince someone of something, you must first establish your credibility, or, in other words, *you must sell yourself* before you sell your message. If people feel that you are not being reasonable or rational, you do not stand a chance. You must be committed to the ideals and goals of your speech and what you are saying. Do not use words such as *maybe* or *might*—use positive words such as *will* and *must*.

You are the authority figure in this speech; in order to seem knowledgeable, you had better supply enough information to prove your points, and you had better know your material cold. People can usually spot someone who is trying to wing a speech. You should also appear to be truthful—even when you are really stretching a point. If you do not appear to be earnest, even if your message is the 100% truth, people will doubt your word and tune out your speech.

Last, do not be afraid to show a little emotion; this is not a sterile or static speech. Your body and voice must match the tone of your words. If your language is strong, you must present a physical force to go along with your delivery.

IMPORTANT AREAS OF PRESENTATION

1. Body language. Make sure that you have a proper posture. If your shoulders are sagging and your legs are crossed, you will not appear as being sincere and people just will not accept your message.

2. Articulation. This refers to how your total vocal process works. There are several steps to this entire process. First, you need air from the lungs, your vocal cords in your larynx must be working, your mouth and tongue must be in sync, and you have to make sure that you have got some saliva in your mouth to keep things oiled. You should be aware of your physical makeup in order to understand how you speak.

3. Pronunciation. Pronounce each word. Avoid slang, except to make a point, and do not slur your words. Avoid saying "you know."

4. Pitch. The highs and lows of your voice are the pitch. Whatever you do, avoid a monotone!

5. Speed. Your speed or pace is an important variable to control. Between 140 and 160 words per minute is the normal pace for a persuasive speech. Any faster and you may appear to be glib; any slower and you sound as if you are lecturing. If you are not sure about your speed, tape yourself for one minute and then replay it and count the number of words you used in the minute. The human ear and brain can compile and decode over 400 spoken words per minute, so if you are going too slow, your listeners' minds are going to start to wander as their brains find other ways to keep themselves occupied.

6. Pauses. These caesurae are a critical, persuasive tool. When you want to emphasize a certain word, just pause for one second before; this highlights the word. If you really want to punch it, pause before and after the word.

7. Volume. Another good tool for persuasive budget speeches is one you should adjust with caution. If you scream all the way through your speech, people will become accustomed to it, and it will lose its effectiveness. On the other hand, a few well-timed shouts can liven up the old speech! Try to project or throw your voice out over the entire group— speak to the last row.

8. Quality. Your voice is gauged by the overall impact that it has on your listeners. Quality of voice is the net caliber of your voice, its character and attributes. Try to keep your vocal quality high; it is what separates your voice from everyone else's.

9. Variance. Controlling vocal elements is your most important consideration of all. Try to change your pitch, volume, and speed at least once every 30 seconds, if only for just one word. Never go more than one paragraph without a vocal variance. This keeps your group locked into your speech, if for no other reason than it sounds interesting. Let the words speak for themselves; reflect their nature through your voice. If you say the word *heave,* let the group feel the onomatopoeic force behind it. If you say the word *bulldozer,* make it sound like a titan earthmover, not like a baby with a shovel.

"Leaky" Speakers

How can people tell when someone is stretching the truth or trying to confuse them? Some people watch the speaker's face, but the problem here is that most people who are used to being confusing can control their faces and their eyes. Smart audiences look further for other signs. Therefore what you have to do is avoid showing any signs of **leaks.** A leak is a subconscious physical imperfection that can signal attempts at being less than honest. Some classic leaks are

- Nervous feet and hands
- Pressing a dubious issue
- Body language incongruous to the speech
- Smiling a great deal
- Constantly complimenting the audience
- A fast delivery

Budgets do not pass very often when supported by leaky speakers.

12

Asking for Support

Speaking Before New Curriculum Meetings

CREATING STAKEHOLDERS

While this book is not a marketing resource, knowing a little bit about the strategies advertising agencies use to promote a product can help you when you are trying to have people support your curricular changes and improvements. The major goal of this speech is to point out how your wonderful, new curriculum will benefit each member of your audience. It is in a very real way much like selling a product. Therefore the most important issue to convey is the message that the listeners are vital members, or stakeholders, of your educational community and that they have a direct responsibility for the quality of your school's instruction. This message will serve to make them a part of your team, even if they have valid concerns.

CREATING A NEED

The first step toward selling a curricular improvement, such as ordering new books or computers, is to get your listeners mentally attuned to your curricular improvement, or to focus their attention on your curricular improvement. The most critical step here is to create a need. People will not support things that they *want* very often, so you must convince them that they and the school *need* your curricular improvement (even if they may not think so at first). When home video-recorder machines first came on the market, millions of dollars were spent trying to convince people that they actually needed this product. The tactic worked, since now millions of homes have VCRs.

Next, determine your objectives by answering these questions:

- What kind of speech is needed?
- What should I wear?
- What age group am I addressing?
- What is my theme?
- What visual aids can I use?
- How long should I speak, and what is my group's motivation for even listening to me?
- What is my most effective approach to reach my group?
- How can the curricular improvement benefit my audience?

Speech Methods

There are the three basic speech methods for selling an improvement to your curriculum—in order, they are:

- Balance your curricular improvement to the current curricula. Show how yours is superior, but never disparage what your school has now.

- Point out new improvements to an old curricular improvement: "If you liked our theater program before, you'll love it now with these new additions."
- Show how your new curricular improvement meets the listeners' basic needs: "We all have computer programming problems now and then; that's why. . ."

Is the Price Always Right?

Keep in mind for most presentations that the price of your curricular improvement will not be the most important issue for your listeners. It is reasonable to assume that your listeners already have a good idea what your improvement's price looks like, so they are interested in the other intangibles you can bring to them. Some of these intangibles include the kind of services that it can offer them; what kind of track record and history your curricular improvements have; is there anything in it for them as individuals (e.g., having cars serviced in an auto repair class); and how easy it will be for the listeners, students, and teachers to make use of your curricular improvement or services.

Control Your Variables

Think of this speech as a one-sided debate. You can give all the positive information that you want, and nobody can argue with you. So choose your facts and information judicially; give only the particulars that bolster your curricular improvement.

Be Creative

Offer advantages of your curricular improvement over the status quo, think up some new sales tactics, and be as creative as you can. However, be sure to include the basics as described in this section.

13

If You Need to Speak on a Moment's Notice

Speaking Before Impromptu Parent Meetings

EXTEMPORANEOUS SPEAKING PROCEDURES AND TACTICS

The ability to speak extemporaneously (to extemp)—or to stand on your own two feet, process information quickly, and make a delivery on the spot—is a valuable life skill and a survival-based commodity for existence in school and business. Almost every professional must extemp briefly in one form or another every day. However, if you are asked to make a full presentation to parents or any other group at the last minute, the skills necessary for success take on a whole new meaning.

The essential difference between an extemporaneous or an **impromptu speech** and a speech where you have had ample preparation time is that you must strive to involve the group in your speech. You must speak *to* them, not *at* them.

HINTS ON DELIVERY

- Begin with an engaging story, germane to the topic, that will be of interest to your listeners.
- Be sure to quickly formulate an exact speech-focusing statement (see Chapter 3) and follow its order in your speech.
- Make *I* statements ("I believe that . . . ," "I want you to understand that. . .").
- Pose hypothetical questions.
- Use metaphors that relate to the listeners' backgrounds.
- Sell yourself.
- Don't be afraid to smile.
- Be relaxed and natural.
- Strive to develop eye contact.
- Develop a rapport with the listeners.
- Give a smooth delivery. Do not try to rattle off data or shotgun facts.

Group Relations

In an extemporaneous speech, your information is vital, but your relationship with the listeners is even more critical. Most of your listeners will understand that you have not had enough time to prepare your materials, so they will focus more on your presentation.

Be sure to constantly monitor your listeners' eyes. If they start to drift off during a section, assume that they are not interested in this section and move along until they are paying attention again.

CHECKLIST FOR PUBLIC-SPEAKING ESSENTIALS

In any speech you give, but especially in an impromptu or extemporaneous speech, focusing on the public-speaking essentials is crucial to your success.

Kinesthesis is the word used here to describe your total physical makeup—your gestures, facial expressions, posture, hands, and so on. You will learn that you have to keep all these bodily components under control, especially when under the gun. It is not as impossible as it may seem—if you get off to a good start. Here is a checklist of rules for speech-making. If you can master these basics, you will be miles ahead of many others who try to make a speech:

1. Never, never start right in on your speech when you reach the podium. Look over your group; try to establish eye contact with everyone. This is called scanning your audience. Count to five, and then go. Remember, **scan** first, and then begin.

2. If some individuals are not looking at you, just smile and stare right at them. Someone else will nudge them to attention.

3. Right before you begin, take a good breath through your nose. Do not open your mouth to breathe since this looks like a false start.

4. Do not make your first words *okay, umm,* or *unnn.* Also, try to avoid saying *well* first. This works only if you were a president in the 1980s.

5. Do not click. Some speakers have this uncanny habit of clicking their tongues when they take a breath. Listen to a recording of yourself speaking, or ask someone else to listen for it to determine if you do this. It happens when the front part of your tongue is pressed against the front of the roof of your mouth, and then you pull your tongue down and away making a *tsssk* sound. Usually, once you become aware of the fact that you are doing this, you can consciously adjust away from clicking.

6. Kinesthesis: Watch you hands; keep them on the podium or behind your back or at your side and absolutely out of your pockets. Keep your feet solidly on the floor. Do not touch your face. Try to stand straight. You might even try to smile a little.

7. Don't take a mental pause by saying *ahhh, you know*, or *okay*. If you must take cerebral rest, say, "All right, then." It sounds more intelligent.

8. Be sure to say thank you at the very end.

9. Do not rush back to your chair. After you say thank you, take a final, three-second scan.

10. For normal speeches, when you have a prepared text, do yourself a favor and memorize the first few lines of your introduction. This helps to establish rapport.

11. This technique is a bit old-fashioned, but in formal situations, you may want to begin your speech with a **salutation,** such as, "Mister Chairman, distinguished friends and colleagues, Mom and Dad . . ." If you do use this salutatory opening, remember to prioritize your salutation starting with whoever is generally regarded as the most-important person listening in the audience. For example, "Boys and girls, street vendors, friends, and Mister Prime Minister" would not go over very well in Toronto.

FAMILIAR GROUND

The most critical thing to remember when delivering an off-the-cuff speech is to quickly get onto familiar ground. Make your topic their topic. How? Try to think of something you know about that would fit the topic. Talking about something you do know something about is better than talking about something that is unfamiliar to you. Tell a funny story. Recite some lines from a play that you know. Talk about your cooking class. Say anything to get on familiar ground. The key here is your segues, which are covered in Chapter 21. Remember that it is only when people do not know what they are talking about that they will stall and stumble.

14

How to Field Questions From Your Audience

Speaking Before Sports Informational Meetings

ANSWERING QUESTIONS

Under normal circumstances, sports or athletic informational meetings offer good opportunities for the athletic director and the coaches to talk about their students and their seasons. The format for this kind of speech follows the traditional speech-to-inform pattern described in Chapter 15. However, this kind of meeting usually involves a question-and-answer period.

If you are willing to accept questions, you need to keep a few strategies in mind.

Most people will ask straightforward questions dealing with the specifics of the sport or of the meeting, so you had best become an expert on your team or program before you speak. When someone from the audience asks a question, you need to repeat it so everyone hears it. In addition, as a way to put the question into terms you can work with, always remember to repeat the question in your own words before you answer it. You can say, "What I hear you asking is. . ."

You will want to be as informative as possible with your answers, but try to keep from turning your answers into marathons. Coaches are rightfully very proud of their athletes and can speak longer than needed at times.

ANSWERING TROUBLESOME QUESTIONS

Sometimes a question will come in that you are not ready for, or you will get a question that could turn your response into a debate. Here are some tips for dealing with troublesome questions:

■ Say, "I don't know, " if you do not know an answer—just admit it! Some speakers will try to snow their way through or give a trite answer, but this can only serve to ruin a good meeting. People will understand if you say, "I don't know."

■ Paraphrase. This is a good technique because you simply repeat the question (as you would do anyway) but in your own words. You will want to rephrase the question as one for which you have an answer ready to go. For a model of this, watch a political press conference someday; speakers there are masters of this maneuver.

■ Agree with the person by saying, "You're right, this is a concern." You have acknowledged the person's interest and validated the importance of the question. Once you do this, you can then spin it off in any direction you want (try to paraphrase "I don't know" or any of the other tactics listed here).

■ Mirror the question. Psychologists have used this approach for years—answer a question with a question. If you feel that a question was asked with a hidden agenda behind it (such as to make you look like a fool), just turn the tables on the questioner. All you have to do is to present the questioner with the null version of the original question. For example: "Do you really think that the team buses are safe?" You respond, "Why do you think that team buses are not safe?"

■ Refer to a higher source. What this means is that it would be inappropriate for you to answer a question that should be referred to a higher source: "Well, that question should be answered by our business manager."

As a final thought on answering questions, remember that most of the questions that you receive you will be able to handle with no problems at all. However, if something does go wrong and the above methods do not work, never lose your temper. Invite the people to stay after the meeting and offer to discuss it with them basketball style: one-on-one.

Speaking Before Parent-Teacher-Student Association Groups

15

Creating a Speech to Inform

Informational Presentations

Basic Speech Organization Skills

So, it's your turn to address the Parent-Teacher-Student Association (PTSA). Be sure to mention all the great things that are happening in your school. But before you do, make sure that you have a well-organized speech.

Several famous speakers have commented on what the most important thing to remember for effective public speaking is: "Tell 'em what you're going to tell 'em; tell 'em; and then tell 'em what you told 'em."

As simple as this may sound, this is the format for the typical deductive public speech: the introduction (tell 'em what you are going to tell 'em); the body (tell 'em); and the conclusion (tell 'em what you told 'em). It is important to explore the nature of these three speech elements.

CATCHING THE LISTENERS' INTEREST

To catch the PTSA's interest, you may want to try a few techniques. You could ask a rhetorical question ("Is this a great school or what?"). On the other hand, you could start with a short story that will pull the listeners in, such as a small narrative about a student taking a difficult test. It really does not matter what technique you use to attract the listeners as long as you follow two basic rules:

1. The story or question you choose is germane to your topic.

2. You should finish the story or answer your question in your conclusion.

Moving Down the Funnel

Once you have everyone's attention, you next move your introduction toward your exact topic. Most speakers give a general background of the topic. For example, if you were a student giving a speech about World War II in history class, you might want to discuss wars in general with such elements as arms and planes and strategy. Then, once you have set the stage, you can begin to tighten the aspects about World War II, which will be included in the body of the speech. For example, if your topic is still World War II, you might find it a bit difficult to cover every facet of the war. What you have to do is to zoom in on three or four of the basic areas of World War II, such as the air war, naval battles, and the major weapons used. Of course, not that you should think of the PTSA as a tactical foe, but it still helps to be prepared.

Think of the process as a funnel on top of a bottle. You start with a wide discussion at the top and then constrict your discussion, sliding down to the specifics of your topic. By the time you hit the neck of the funnel, the audience knows exactly where you are heading and what the elements of your topic will be.

Finally, once you are sliding down the neck of the funnel and have announced the specifics of your speech, you deliver your speech-focusing statement. The speech-focusing statement is where you "tell 'em what you're going to tell 'em." The speech-focusing statement is explained in Chapter 3.

After you have your introduction, you have to move along to the meat of your speech—the body. The body tells all the facts and explains all the details of your speech-focusing statement. You should be very careful to follow the pattern as outlined in your introduction. If in your introduction you tell your listeners that you are going to discuss issues A, B, and C, then you must discuss A, B, C, not B, C, A or C, B, A.

While the order of your topics is an important issue, the logical design and construction you employ are equally important. In other words, what reasoning did you use for ordering your speech? Are you showing how something developed over time? Are you explaining why something happened in school the way it did? Are you detailing how to do something?

SPEECH CONSTRUCTION METHODS

To answer these concerns, there are several logical patterns you can follow when designing your speech. Some of the most obvious methods for construction are as follows:

■ **Trace.** Show the exact steps involved in how your topic came or should come about.

■ **Define and differ.** First, place your topic into its class (e.g., a koala is an animal that lives in a tree). Next, show how your topic differs from all other members of its class (the koala differs from all other tree-dwelling animals because it lives in Australia, is a marsupial, has thick, gray fur, and does television commercials).

■ **Process.** Show how something is done or how to do something.

■ **Problem solving.** Show how to address a specific or general concern about something.

■ **Describe.** Describe your topic with details, trying to create a mood for your listeners. This style works well when talking about out-of-the-ordinary topics (e.g., paint a word picture to affect the listeners' emotions. If there was a fire in the neighborhood, describe the searing heat and the blue-red fire rather than just listing the factual details).

Methods of Presentation

Once you have decided on the logical development of your topic, you can consider some of the various methods to present the order of your ideas:

- *Chronological order.* Describe the time order in which events took place.
- *Cause to effect.* Show how your topic was the result of essential events.
- *Climax order.* Work from the least important information to the most important.
- *Anticlimax order.* Work from the most to least important information.
- *Spatial order.* Describe the physical setup of your topic.

Finally, you move to your conclusion. To begin, never say, "in conclusion" or "at last" in your speech. This gives the listener permission to tune you out. It is a much better idea to simply restate your introduction and tell the PTSA why it was important that they listened and what you want them to do or to get out of the presentation.

CONCLUSIONS AND ENDGAME

The most important consideration in your conclusion is your endgame. The idea behind an endgame is to leave the listeners thinking about your speech, or to leave the listeners with one last thought. Here are some suggestions:

- Finish the story you started in the introduction.
- Answer your rhetorical question.
- End with a rhetorical quotation.
- Pose a final question to challenge your listeners' intellect.

FINDING AND PREPARING DATA

An informative speech about your school must have both quantitative and qualitative support data: In other words, there must be a lot of good information. The first thing you have to do is gather as much raw information as possible. There are three Bs to finding and preparing your data:

■ *Brainstorm.* Sit down and just write every idea on the topic that pops into your mind. After you have a large enough list, select the better ones for further consideration.

■ *Bag your ammo.* Get all the information you can: facts, statistics, quotations, observations, interviews, and so forth. Talk with the other teachers, principals, and school administrators. If you are talking about events outside the school, you will want to check out the Internet, encyclopedias, dictionaries, newspapers, newsmagazines, a thesaurus, guides to periodicals, almanacs, and atlases. And by all means, make use of the best source of information known to humankind: librarians—they love to help!

■ *Busy-bee-active.* If you do not spend enough time looking and asking, you may miss some of the most critical information available. Spend the time necessary to do a good job.

FINAL PREPARATIONS

- Review your material once again.
- Reread your notes.

■ Create a basic outline.

■ Get your supporting ammunition from the library, a teacher, a parent, a friend, or, perhaps, the Internet: graphs, findings, quotes, examples, historical details, famous speeches, original documents, and so on.

■ Write and deliver the speech. Always use legal pads for writing and delivering your speech; it looks professional, and besides, cards can be dropped and become mixed up, and other kinds of paper just look messy. If you prefer to use a computer printout, consider taping the pages to legal-pad paper.

■ In your presentation, never apologize. Some people say things like, "Well, this isn't too good, but. . ."

■ Avoid saying, "I think" and "I feel." Take a position and stand by it.

RECURSIVE WORDS AND AMPHIBOLES

This is a good chance to really express yourself, so make your words exact, and avoid fluff. Also, avoid **recursive** words, which are words that define each other and never really reveal their meanings, such as defining *oculist* by saying *ophthalmologist*, and then defining *ophthalmologist* by saying *oculist*. Another variation of recursive or **circular language** is when the definition of a word includes a variation of the word being defined, such as defining *goodness* as a state of being good.

You should also stay away from amphiboles, which are phrases that can be misunderstood due to poor grammar, ambiguity, or lack of an antecedent (e.g., "I sat by my wife singing."). So, who is doing the singing?

Finally, again, try to memorize the first and last few lines of your introduction and your conclusion, because it leaves a strong first and last impression.

AVOIDING MALAPROPISMS

Watch for slang, and a **malapropism** or **spoonerism.** As for slang, any time in a speech you say, "You know," you are in trouble. "You know" is deadly to a speaker's credibility.

Malapropisms are named after Mrs. Malaprop, a character in Richard Brinsley Sheridan's play *The Rivals.* A malapropism is an incorrect word or words that are humorous in the context in which they are misused. Think of some of the things Yogi Berra would say. Spoonerisms are named for the Reverend William Spooner, Dean of New College, Oxford, who would unintentionally transpose the initial sounds of two words in a sentence; for example, "It is *kisstomary* to *cuss* the bride."

Both these may reveal something about what you as the speaker are really thinking, as does a Freudian slip. For example, it's a Freudian slip if you have a golf game to attend later that day and during your speech about paper manufacturing and paper supplies for your school, you say, "From the trees, you get your three-wood, I mean, wood, to produce your paper stock for the new standardized tests." But if you are a nongolfer who isn't concerned with golf on any level and you make the same slip, it's a malapropism.

16

Presenting Yourself and Your Speech

Board Meetings—Reporting on Students' Progress

COMMUNICATION SKILLS

Every now and again, you might be asked to speak before the board to report on student events or some similar topic. The board will be very interested in your topic, so for this kind of speech, you should focus on your communication skills in order to make the best impression possible.

All living things communicate; you cannot not communicate. Even the smallest microorganisms can send messages to each other. Albeit they can't order a pizza on the telephone, they can still signal basic needs and wants to each other.

Interpersonal Communication

Humans communicate via a process known as **interpersonal communication.** One interpretation of this term is that *inter* means *between* and *personal* comes from the Latin word for a mask used by actors, the *persona.* Interpersonal communication is literally the mask we all wear for each other.

Speaking before the board, you must be careful that your mask reflects what is really going on inside your brain and not what you think people would like to see. The etymology above of *interpersonal* gives you **clues** on how to proceed.

To keep your mask in proper shape, you should take care to appear sincere—sincere in language and in physical appearance. Take the time to make sure that you are ready to go—check your tie or hair or dress. Is your speech prepared as well as it could be? Did you make sure that the speech reads well?

Remember, you cannot appear to be sincere if people don't accept you, even if you're trying your hardest. If you have the best speech in the world and you are dressed like a ne'er-do-well, no matter how sincere you try to be, nobody will listen. Your mask is your total appearance and what you do with it.

Dressing for the Part

You must be careful when you accept a speaking engagement such as this to make sure that you have a good understanding of the nature of the event. Ask the person who is acting as your contact what the dress and nature of the event will be.

For example, if you are being asked to speak at a charity event and you discover that it is being held at a fancy country club and everyone will be dressed in tuxedos, it would behoove you to make sure that your dress is equally as formal. If it is not, you will have alienated some of your audience before you even open your mouth. The converse is true as well. If the occasion is informal and you overdress, people will feel just as uncomfortable. If you do not normally attend board meetings, be sure to ask how to dress.

Dress the way your audience will dress, or a touch above. When in doubt, tend toward the conservative. If you start to research the effects of color on people, you will notice that people who wear dark suits or dresses do so to emphasize their confidence and power. It is held that people dressed in red or wearing red ties or suspenders radiate action and energy.

No matter how many words you speak, most of the message received from a public speech is nonverbal. Therefore it is critical that you can be seen during your speech, which is where good grooming comes into play. If you have long hair that normally covers part of your face, consider pulling it back for your speech. Beards need to be well trimmed so that even the people in the back row can see if you are smiling or grimacing. Make sure that you have a nonverbal plan in place for your dress. Ensure that you understand what the message behind your dress will be before you take the microphone; know how the audience will react, and do not leave anything to chance.

OVERSHINING

A word about overshining. There will be times when you are asked to make a speech where your role is to introduce or to promote someone else. In many situations, the person you are working with will not have the public-speaking skills that you humbly enjoy. It is very important in these situations that you do not overshine, or upstage, your guest. You may even have to pull back the reins a bit to make sure that you do not steal the spotlight.

CLICHÉS

Another thing to remember about language in any formal speech is to avoid using clichés. Clichés have no real meaning in your speech, can tend to turn off your listeners, and are just substitutes for meaningful descriptive language. Educators are especially critical of a cliché. It is a phrase or saying that most everyone uses, along with the fact that everyone understands the meaning or idea behind the cliché. It is like a verbal shorthand. Here is a list of some of the immortal clichés:

- As if
- What goes around comes around
- Out of the frying pan and into the fire
- Dressed to kill
- Let's do lunch.
- Easier said than done
- Sadder but wiser
- Money is the root of all evil.
- Thick as a brick
- I need feedback.
- Try, try again.
- C'est la vie.
- Personal space
- Nobody is perfect.
- Awesome

MAKING YOUR SPEECH INTERESTING: VARIANCES AND HUMOR

The best barometer of how you are doing is watching the board watching you. If they seem bored, you had better improvise something to snap them back to your speech. Try yelling a few words as if you had planned on it all along. Do anything to get their attention. It is your story, after all; how do they know if you really are not supposed to yell at that point?

If you are really brave, you might want to try to inject some intelligent humor, but be careful. If you are not a humorous person by nature, do not force it. Humor can easily backfire. There is no greater motivation for wanting to crawl into a dark hole on the stage than telling a joke and having nobody laugh; you can mentally hear the crickets chirping in the back row.

Remember that the best humor usually flows from the humorous details of the story itself, not from a canned or prefabricated joke. Listen to some late-night talk shows, and watch how the pros do it. It is not easy.

Humor has a way of delivering a very real message without actually coming out and saying what you mean, especially when telling stories about students. These are some of the gray areas of language and communication, using devices such as innuendo and allusions. Most successful humor relies on the listener being able to read between the lines.

Successful humor is much more than simple slams, insults, sarcasm, or put-downs. Engaging humor is based in both school reality and understandable humor. Sometimes you laugh so that you do not cry.

Think of good humor as being a verbal thump to your listeners' heads, a humorous wake-up call about an issue or a person. Again, the only limit is that the listeners must get it.

For example, if you made a humorous reference to your authoritarian, dog-owning, next-door neighbor when you were a child as being "a very dogmatic person," you might think that it is endlessly funny; however, it is doubtful that any of your audience would get it.

V

Speaking Before Collegial Groups

17

Beyond Words—How to Use Visual and Other Aids

National or State Conferences

How to Use Visual and Other Aids

Presenting before a national or state conference can be a high-point of your career. Nothing is more fulfilling than being appreciated by your colleagues. Addressing team-faculty-staff meetings is also an important occasion. When making your presentation, you will almost certainly need visual aids. However, make sure that your aids help and do not hinder your presentation. You cannot take any visual aid for granted.

An ancient Chinese proverb states that a picture is worth a thousand words, which probably is not accurate, since they did not have computers back then to perform the arithmetical computations. Nevertheless, pictures and visual aids should save you at least a few hundred breaths at a conference.

To be effective when you use visual aids, you need to have your hands free most of the time. To make this happen, you should have your speech either memorized or in an outline form so you can use your hands to point and gesture.

As you use your visual aids to emphasize or explain your topic, remember the acronym often used by professional speechmakers: KISS (keep it simple and straightforward)—so everyone gets it. The idea being that you may be tempted to meander on about complicated details because now you have a visual aid. The visual aid should be kept simple and direct and used only to reinforce your message.

One final word on your script—this is true for every speech you will ever make—take a photocopy of it if it is hand-written, or copy it to a floppy disk if it is on your computer, and store it separately from the original. You may lose a speech only once in your lifetime, but that once will make copying it worthwhile.

Why Use Visual Aids?

Visual aids are used to enhance what you have to say to your audience. Briefly, visual aids need to be colorful and simple. They do not replace you or your words; they are merely tools you use in your communication efforts. Visual aids are very effective sensory tools when used to support the opening to your speech, when you need to explain complex issues, when you present statistics, or when you need to focus your audience's thinking on a topic.

Issues for Visual Aids

You need to use visual aids very carefully. First, you should be sure to practice your speech using the aids several times before you go live. Make sure that the aid is not a distraction by pulling the audience's attention away from you and to the bells and whistles of the aid. Keep to the point. In addition, when you arrive at your speaking location, if possible, perform a dry run with the aids to make sure everything is working properly. Most important, when you have finished using the visual aid, turn it off and put it away, or it will distract your audience.

Always make sure you have a backup plan when it comes to your visual aids. Things can, and often do, go wrong. If you are using a computer-based aid, you should make overhead transparencies and have a projector ready just in case your projector goes out or the laptop freezes. Descriptions of visual and other aids follow.

Handouts. Photocopy the basics of your speech and hand them out *after* your presentation. If you are delivering a speech supported by a computer-based medium, make sure that you copy and print out each of the cells from your presentation. These are excellent for your listeners to refer to after your speech. As opposed to the aforementioned parent back-to-school night presentation, this time, be sure to hand out paperwork after your speech. If you hand out the bulk of your materials before or during your speech, your audience will be tempted to tune out your voice and start reading for themselves. Remember that the human mind can process information much faster than you can speak it. Therefore reading is a good way for someone to fill in the mental gaps.

Models. Make a scale model of your topic and use it to illustrate various physical aspects of the specifics of your speech. These are very practical tools, especially if your topic is something too large to carry, such as the Statue of Liberty.

Transparencies. Your transparencies or overheads can detail complicated issues as you sequentially move through your stacks. They are reusable and travel well (be sure to put sheets of paper between your transparencies). Make sure that you put only essential ideas on the transparency and that you speak extemporaneously from the sheet—do not read verbatim from the transparency itself. Be sure to use a sheet of paper that covers the material below where you are working on the transparency; otherwise, people will tend to read ahead and ignore what you are saying at the moment. In addition, while you prepare the transparencies ahead of time, you can leave some sheets blank so you can fill in some key words as you move along your speech to add emphasis.

Maps. Create a vividly colored map if your topic needs a geographic perspective. If you remember to limit the amount of lines and names on the map (KISS), you will discover that a map is a good tool for a discussion.

Illustrations. There is no tool more effective for driving home a point than a well-prepared, humorous drawing. It must be intelligent and clever if it is going to work properly.

Graphs. Graphs, charts, and diagrams should be large enough to be seen by everyone in the room. They should be clear and easy to understand (KISS). Graphs are used to show how your topic relates to another variable. For example, if your topic is "the value of an education," you might want to plot "amount of education" as the ordinate on your graph and "income" as the abscissa. Graphs are used to show the relative degree of your topic using three popular styles: the bar graph, the pie graph, and the line graph. You should check with your encyclopedia to find out which type of graph would best fit your needs. Different situations, different topics, and different materials call for different types of graphs.

Flip Charts. Flip charts work well as aids for speeches. You can prepare them ahead of time and just fill in some key words as you move along your speech, or you can write lightly in pencil on the chart, giving yourself some invisible notes that you fill in as you speak. Use large and colorful letters, put only one theme or thought on a single page, and use no more than 10 lines on a page. Finally, make sure that everyone in the room has a clear line of sight to the flip chart—you may have to put it on a table or find some way to lift it to eye level for everyone.

Microphones. This is one aid you should practice with a good deal before you begin your speech. Most people are unaccustomed to using any kind of microphone, and it shows during their speeches. Know ahead of time that things can and will go wrong. Even though you made sure to check the volume and sound quality before you started your speech (please say something other than "testing, testing"), your first few words might boom or squeak across the room, and you should be ready to react if this happens. Ask that the volume be turned down if you are getting a feedback sound. Move away from the microphone. See if the wires are connected properly. If nothing else works and nobody sprints to your rescue, turn off the microphone and do the best you can under the circumstances. Unfortunately, this is also the time when your speech anxiety is at its highest, and if you are not mentally prepared for a potential problem, it could begin a negatively spiraling self-perception.

Video Clips. Showing a brief clip from a film can be a very powerful presentational tool. The obvious drawback is that you have to carry the equipment around. If you decide to show a clip, be sure to tell the audience what to look for during the presentation. This focus for viewing will help them actively zero in on your specifics instead of passively watching. And don't forget to obtain any permissions that may be needed.

Slides. This could be your most expensive option because of the developing expenses; however, slides can act as a superb vehicle for presenting your lecture or demonstration. With slides, you can whisk your group off to Egypt or into the guts of a nuclear reactor. Make sure that your slides are in the proper order and that you practice your timing with the projector.

White Boards. Using a white board or blackboard is not a strong visual aid for a formal speech. You have to turn your back on your audience, and it seems slow in today's hurry-up world. Use a board only if you need to answer a question by illustrating an answer. Even then, it would be better to use a blank transparency and draw on the screen.

COMPUTER-BASED MEDIA PRESENTATIONS

Using a laptop in conjunction with a projector has become the most popular form of visual aid. While it is used more in the business world than in schools, many teachers, principals, and school administrators are discovering the benefits of having these presentational tools. Many forms of software are available for presentations, and you should take the time to research which one will work best for you. Again, the only caveat is to make sure that everything is set up well ahead of time and given a dry run. Finally, make sure you have a backup plan. As noted above, you should make overhead transparencies and have an overhead projector ready just in case your computer projector goes out or the laptop freezes.

The basic rule is that computer-based media presentations should be succinct, colorful, and playful. In an age in which audiences are very much accustomed to sound bites as substitutes for full-length discourse, you must resist the temptation to use a full libretto when a few expressions would suffice to make your point.

You should be certain that if you are going to go to the trouble and expense of using computer-based media that you make sure that you use them as effectively as possible. Ask yourself some preliminary questions, and if the answers come back as no, you should consider another form of presentation. Ask yourself if the media will actively engage your audience. Ask yourself if the media will support your message and not take it over and become an end unto themselves. Ask yourself if the media will be easy to follow for the audience. If you feel comfortable with your answers, you can then use this checklist to make sure that you have everything in place for your presentation. As a note, if you are employing a performance assessment such as a rubric for this speech, you can easily use some of these as criteria for your assessment:

- Does the presentation run well without problems 100% of the time during practice?
- Does the presentation fulfill its content requirements, giving the audience enough support information?
- Does the presentation have at least seven slides or view screens?
- Does the presentation use consistent text that is grammatically correct?
- Does the presentation have slides or view screens that are organized in a logical fashion?
- Does the presentation use and give credit to various resources?
- Does the presenter know how to use the technology effectively?
- Does the presentation have at least two colorful charts, clip arts, or photos?
- Does the presentation not try to impress the audience with sounds and spinning words or other bells and whistles?
- Does the presentation have a clear introduction, body, and conclusion so that it tells a story?
- Does the presentation reinforce the speaker's attempt at the end of the speech to motivate the audience to act?

ABOMINABLE WORDS

Now that you have these visual aids, you should take care to make sure that your spoken words do not embarrass you. Here is a list of speakers' abominable words—words that can trip up even a seasoned veteran:

- *A lot* versus *alot*. Say *a lot* as two words meaning *a great number*. *Alot* does not exist.

- *Almost* versus *most*. *Almost* is an adverb (I almost gave a good speech). *Most* is an adjective (Most speeches are fun!).
- *Beside* versus *besides*. *Beside* means next to something. *Besides* means in addition to.
- *Good* versus *well*. *Good* is an adjective (He is a good speaker.). *Well* is a predicate adjective or an adverb (She speaks well.).
- *Hanged* versus *hung*. People are *hanged*. Pictures are *hung*.
- *His* and *her* versus *their*. Use of personal pronouns in speeches requires *her* or *his*, or *he* or *she* for singular reference.
- *Irregardless* versus *regardless*. *Irregardless* is a double negative—use *regardless*.
- *Lay* versus *lie*. People *lie* down today and *lay* down yesterday; things are *laid* down.
- *Ourself* versus *ourselves*. *Ourself* does not exist; use the reflexive pronoun *ourselves*.
- *Sit* versus *set*. People *sit*; things are *set*.

18

Leading a Staff or Inservice Meeting

Team, Faculty, and Staff Meetings

SHARING

Depending on the nature of your routine team, faculty, or staff meetings, planning can go a long way in ensuring a smooth and successful meeting. Teachers do not object to spending their time in a meeting as long as they feel it is time well spent. Usually, there is a laundry list of issues that you will need to get through, and you need to attend to business first. However, the hallmark of a successful faculty meeting is having time set aside for talking and for listening. Be sure to designate a portion of the meeting to listening to what everyone has to say. People might want to ask questions, tell success stories, share concerns, extend accolades to each other, talk about students, or whatever else is important at that moment. However, if you don't put aside time for the sharing, this kind of communication will not take place, and your meetings will become known as being very one-sided.

ROLE-PLAYING

For longer staff meetings or inservices, before you turn to the business at hand, as a method for breaking the ice and establishing trust and rapport among your colleagues, consider a role-playing activity as your warm-up strategy.

Role-playing has become extremely popular in the past few years. Role-playing is regarded as a critical developmental activity in formal training programs for almost every professional occupation. You can play out various scenarios that could occur in the real world, and then step back and analyze what worked and what did not work in the safety of your own learning environment. Role-playing has also become enormously popular in computer and Internet games, as many people enjoy acting out ideas without actually putting themselves in harm's way. Role-playing is an important skill to develop as you progress as a public speaker, since many speeches in real life involve role-playing in one form or another.

Role-playing is a way of telling a story in which you play a central character. The story has a basic skeletal outline at the beginning, but it is up to you and your peers to decide where the story's plot line goes from there. You and your peers will develop a story in which each person portrays a character in a plot that is unfolding in front of you. In role-playing, you adopt a personality other than your own, which means that you are free to be as expressive as you wish without revealing any of your own personal feelings.

Not surprisingly, most people prefer role-playing games that involve a narrative that has some kind of danger attached to it. Role-playing an action-packed trip to the grocery store in the family minivan just doesn't compare to tracking a desperate villain deep in the mysterious tropical forest.

Create a storyline that in some way relates to your situation in your school, but make it an adventure. If your school is having communications issues, try a role-play where everyone is a secret agent attempting to pass along a message that can save the world. Make the objective for the role-play similar to the concern or issue that you wish to address in your meetings.

There is an example of how you can develop a storyline in *Role-Play Exercise—Terror at 10,000 Feet* in Chapter 24.

Speaking Before Community Groups

19

Making Decisions About Your Audience and Your Speaking Environment

Civic Organizations With Community Concerns About Students

PROBLEM SOLVING

Quite often civic groups will invite teachers, principals, and school administrators to speak before their organizations to address areas of general or generic concern. The best approach to take in this situation is to treat their topic in a problem-solving manner.

In any speech to solve a problem situation, there are certain strategies that you should keep in mind:

1. State in your own words the issues that are involved and why it is important that everyone listens to your speech. What are the variables that you can control? What are the variables that you cannot control? Remind the audience that while you work with children, you cannot predict their behavior or take responsibility for their actions.

2. The audience might have read someone's article or have heard someone else's opinion. State what differentiates your position or solution from anyone else's position. Why is your stance unique?

3. List ahead of time your perceptions of your school's strengths and your own weaknesses. Accentuate your strengths and downplay your weaknesses, but remind the audience that school plays only one role in the lives of children.

4. Examine your audience. What do they need and what can you provide to make sure that you are part of a win-win outcome?

5. Choose your words carefully. Use language that befits the situation.

THE EMPTY-SEAT DILEMMA

No matter what your topic, when you are speaking in front of a community group, you need to take some control of the meeting's variables. Be sure to arrive at the meeting room at least 20 minutes before you are scheduled to speak, to become familiar with the room and to make any last-minute adjustments.

One important adjustment is to make sure that there are few if any empty seats. In an unspoken way, it hurts your credibility as the guest speaker if there are many unfilled seats. To deal with this issue in a proactive way, ask your contact to limit the number of seats set up to about half the normal number. It is far better to add chairs as more people come in than it is to have a sea of empty seats.

ARE MORNING, AFTERNOON, OR EVENING MEETINGS BEST?

Each has its particular advantages and disadvantages. In a morning meeting, the audience is usually more focused because the routine issues of the day have not caught up with them yet. This makes morning meetings the best choice to meet with community groups. Be sure to get to your point quickly as you address the full group, and allow some time for small-group discussions to process what you have conveyed.

People who attend afternoon meetings are usually tired and are looking forward to dinner and getting a well-deserved rest. Your job is to make the presentation as active or as hands-on as possible—have handouts ready, or call for questions. Be sure to keep the tempo upbeat and resist any temptation to lecture. For your lunch, be sure to eat a light meal. Heavy lunches take a long time and a lot of energy to digest.

Dinner or evening meetings can be the most difficult for you, especially when there is alcohol involved. When speaking to the community or a group after dinner, be sure to include some elements of entertainment, such as a story or an anecdote. The audience is usually receptive to a speaker for no more than an hour, so keep it brief. Finally, be sure to pass on any alcohol yourself. Alcohol is a depressant and will never improve your performance.

MEMORIZATION ADVICE

As has been noted earlier, obtaining eye contact is important in any speech. When addressing this audience, it is especially important to appear in charge of your topic, and eye contact helps. This section will offer you helpful suggestions on how to memorize a speech. You should always memorize at least parts of the introduction and conclusion of your speech to present a strong opening and closing. People will form a first impression of you within the first 10 seconds, and these first impressions will dictate their appreciation of the rest of your speech.

Memory Supports

Here is a list of memory supports. One may just work for you:

Mnemonics. The cognitive theory of understanding postulates that we tend to clump information bits together in our brains. Therefore if we can make what we want to memorize more mentally sticky, it will be easier to associate and to remember. As a shorthand, try to think up acronyms or silly sayings to help you memorize a difficult passage. "Every good boy does fine" works for music students. Ben Franklin insisted, "Spring ahead, fall back" (This is a joke, just to see if you're paying attention.). The Great Lakes are HOMES. Popular acronyms include "RADAR" for "radio detecting and ranging," and "laser" for "light amplification by stimulated emissions of radiation."

Outline Reduction. First, write out your whole speech. Next, outline it. Then make sure that you can deliver your whole speech from the outline, and, finally, outline the outline. Simply keep cutting down on the structure of the outline until you are left with only a few key words. Memorize the key words, in order, via a mnemonic device.

Mental Photographs. Try to picture the elements of your speech in one figure form. Pretend that you are an artist and that you are painting one big picture of your entire topic. If your topic is the tax system, draw a mental picture of a king holding forms, with people at work around him, handing him a part of their food. This holistic tactic of memorization is very popular among professionals.

When in Doubt, Punt. One last word on memorization. If you forget something, never admit to it. Keep right on going—never go back. Nobody in the room knows your speech—the only way they will find out that you had forgotten something is if you tell them. If you go blank, don't panic, just make it look as if you're taking a reflective pause—take a few steps and make it look as if you're deep in thought (even though your mind is racing for a scrap of help).

Finally—as an extra measure of moving your short-term memory to longer-term memory—after memorizing the night before, try to recall as much as you can the instant you wake up the next morning before you get out of bed. Try it!

20

Sharing Yourself With the Children

Library Story Hour

STORYTELLING ELEMENTS (SHIFTS, DENOUEMENTS, ABSTRACT AND CONCRETE LANGUAGE)

Nothing is more fun than reading aloud to a group of appreciative young people. If you are especially interested in personalizing the experience for the children, consider writing your own story based loosely on an experience that happened to you. If you decide to try this, there are six basic elements of storytelling to remember:

1. Use vivid language. Try to make the children feel the story through your language. Try to find synonyms for dull or nonexact words. Never say *good, nice,* or *varied*; these are tired old words. Try *auspicious, congenial,* and *sundry*. There is nothing wrong with introducing some new vocabulary words for the students—be sure to make a list of the big words you use so their teacher can have a vocabulary sheet for use later. Check your thesaurus and grammar, and rid your story of verbal dinosaurs. Also be sure to use in the story specific details from your memory. What was the setting: time, place, dress, and weather? What were your feelings: happy, sad, melancholy? Human emotions help develop a working theme in a story. Make your story reflect these details.

2. *Be sincere.* As mentioned earlier, the only way that you can make a story come alive is if you are sincere. Look at the obvious logic: You are telling a story about an event that happened somewhere else at some other time. For your story to affect listeners, you have to coax them into suspending reality and stepping into your story. It is the same principle in operation at a theater or at the movies. The audience is sitting in their seats—they are not really climbing a mountain or driving a racecar, but if the story is presented sincerely, the audience will allow themselves to be carried away. Keep this in mind during your presentation. A good story will actually draw in the group. Watch the children's eyes, and you can tell if they are really into your story.

3. *Keep in order.* Make sure that you relate your story in the proper order of events. Nothing sounds worse than someone telling a story and then backing up to fill in a missed event. Keep the story in order, and do not skip around. Another very good thought on this issue is to tell your story in the present tense, or at least use a past participle (e.g., "I am running to the store" as compared with, "I ran to the store.") Having an *ing* at the end of your verb makes the story more immediate and alive.

4. *Have a memorable message.* This should seem obvious. Pick an interesting story. A story about a trip to London is more likely to be interesting than a tale about cleaning your silverware. If you are unsure about your story, try it on someone and note the reaction. Who knows, maybe your silverware fascinates

you but might not be quite as thrilling to others. The best stories not only relate an event but also have a message to them. A story that has a moral to it, or a lesson attached, is more memorable than a story that merely tells events. This is the basic formula for a fable or a parable. "I guess I'll never tell a lie again," is a typical lesson learned.

5. *Shift your plot.* Your story should have a clear beginning, middle, and ending, much the same way a movie does. The beginning tells how you as the narrator became involved in your story; the middle is the bulk of the action; and the ending ties up the loose ends (known as the **denouement**), relates the end to the plot, explains how the story affected your life, and conveys your moral. Most people have an intuitive ability to tell stories, but few know how to move the story from the beginning to the middle, and from the middle to the end. In storytelling, such a transition is known as a **shift.** Every story has two shifts, one in the beginning and one in the middle. The shift is the event that triggers the next section (e.g., "Everything was fine that morning until the brown bear came along."). The shift must occur at the end of the section; it would seem somewhat impractical to jump to the ending halfway through the middle.

6. *Abstract versus concrete language.* There are two basic types of storytelling languages: abstract and concrete. Abstract language is connotative; it suggests rather than describes. It uses a figurative vocabulary (metaphors, similes, etc.) and is used in speeches that deal with feelings or emotions or abstracts. *Love* is an example of an abstract. Concrete language is denotative, it literally describes, and it shows exact meaning. You would use concrete language when describing a person, place, or physical thing. When you say *chair*, everyone knows that you mean a four-legged stool with a back, used for sitting. If you say that you love your chair, then you have successfully mixed both concrete and abstract language. Neither language type is better, but you must be aware enough to use the proper one at the proper time. If you

are talking about a tender memory from your past love life and use concrete language, you may not get your point across effectively to small children (e.g., "As I held her blanch, affable digits and we looked at luna, I pondered osculation.").

DEVELOPING A CHARACTER THROUGH PLOT

Feel free to make your character a mouse or a moose; if you can create personable characters, you can then put them through several exploits, and your listeners will develop sympathy for the characters. Remember, in a good story, the plot is not the most important consideration; the human drama of the character is. The plot is only a vehicle to spotlight your characters.

21

How to Lead and Participate in a Discussion Group

Community Forums or Panel Discussions

Primary Discussion Steps

Leading a discussion usually implies that there is an issue that needs to be addressed and a change that needs to accompany that decision. Change is never easy on people, and the more input they have into the change process, especially when educational issues are involved, the more likely they are to buy into the change when it happens. Without discussing an issue, you take the chance of having people feel alienated and not part of the team. Niccolo Machiavelli summed this up best in *The Prince* (1532): "There is nothing more difficult to take in hand, more perilous to conduct, or more uncertain in its success, than to take the lead in the introduction of a new order to things."

Steps in a Discussion

There are six primary steps in a discussion. Notice that to accomplish some of these steps, some homework must be done. The steps in order are:

1. *Define every word of the resolution.* Everyone should agree on the usage of every word. Discussions can easily bog down if people have different conceptions of key words. Try to avoid *educationize* or other words that are used only by educators.

2. *Study the issue—what is its history?* What factors control it? What caused the problem? Who is to blame?

3. *Shotgun solutions.* Everyone brainstorms ideas rapid fire. One member should write down every solution on a blackboard, or have a recorder write them down.

4. *Eliminate inadequate solutions.* Get rid of obviously defective solutions. A simple majority decision is good enough to reject weak ideas.

5. *Discuss.* This is the heart of your discussion. Take each solution or idea left on the blackboard and discuss its relative strengths and weaknesses. Rank order each successive solution or idea: "Is this new one better or worse than the one before? Where does it fit in a hierarchy from good to best?"

6. *Devise an action plan.* Once you have decided on the best action or solution, create a hypothetical action plan to implement your solution. Be as specific as possible within realistic boundaries.

ROLES OF THE DISCUSSION LEADER

If you are the leader of the discussion, you will be kept busy during this process. The discussion leader should

- Keep the discussion moving along
- Remember that this is not a debate, so the leader encourages cooperation among the group, not conflict
- Make decisions on how to proceed because parliamentary procedures do not apply to a discussion
- Summarize from time to time what has been said and agreed on
- Keep control
- Make sure that everyone participates
- Make final summations
- Make sure everyone agrees with the outcomes

REQUIREMENTS OF THE PARTICIPANTS

If you are a participant in an open discussion, you will be expected to behave like a civilized human being. All it takes is one power-hungry member, and the discussion is in danger. Just as you learned the requirements for a group leader, there are requirements of each participant in a discussion as well. As a participant, you should

- Do your homework
- Be willing to compromise on your pet issues
- Keep an open mind
- Make sure everyone gets a chance to speak and no one monopolizes the discussion
- Attack a person's position but never the person
- Avoid blanket statements (e.g., "You're always wrong.")
- Be consistent in your views and, if you do change your mind, explain why
- Be willing to drop losing arguments
- Be willing to go along with the group's decision because nobody likes a sore loser

GROUP INTERACTION

Take a few minutes to just sit back and watch the process of human decision making and interaction. At times, it can be amusing, and it is always interesting. If you can be objective enough, try to step outside yourself and observe how you are fitting into the whole scheme of things. How do you react to the group, and how do they react to you? If you are not able to do this, ask a friend or someone from your speech study group to take notes on how often you speak, to whom you speak, to whom you respond, and on your general body language and verbal tones.

SEGUES

Moving a meeting along means moving from one topic to another to another. To accomplish this, you need to think about each **segue.** A segue is an immediate transition from one topic to another or from one speaker to another. Segues are what glue talk shows together. "Yes, Jan, donuts are nice, and something else that's nice is a health club, where our cameras visited today . . ." A segue allows a story or program to flow without any abrupt shifts.

There are two conditions of segues: their styles and the key words employed. The styles of segues are

- Full segue—there is no doubt that you are going on to a new topic: "Our next topic is the farm and its impact on rural economies."
- Half segue—a gentler shift: "Meanwhile, back at the farm . . ."
- Key word segue—jumps into a new topic but pulls down a key word from the previous topic: "Today, the prices are up all across the board, just as on the farm . . ."

Key Words

If you are employing a key word segue, there are several elements and conditions to consider, the most important of which are the key words that you repeat from the previous sentence in your new topic.

- If you want to show time shifts, try these words: *next, meanwhile, later.*
- If you want to show that you are going on to another thought, try *also, besides, moreover.*
- If you want to show contrast, try *on the other hand, otherwise, similarly.*
- If you want to indicate location changes, try *nearby, across the river, adjacent to.*
- If you want to point out results, try *thus, therefore, as a result.*
- If you want to show that a conclusion has been reached, try *as we have seen, looking overall.*

Note: Do not say, "In conclusion," when you have actually reached your conclusion; this gives listeners permission to tune you out.

VII

When All
Else Fails

22

Speaking When You Really Cannot Say Anything

Nine Tactics to Use When None of the Conventional Wisdom Works

If you are reading this section, you are probably in a situation where none of the conventional wisdom offered before has worked. Perhaps for personnel, security, or privacy reasons, you cannot say anything about the designated topic. Or perhaps you were asked a question that you cannot answer because it involves an issue of confidentiality. However, you are still being asked to make a speech, and you have to deliver in some way.

This being the case, experiment with various tactics. Try adding some of these ingredients into the mix if you want to leave your audience satisfied that you made a speech or answered a question, even when you cannot say too much. These tactics follow:

1. Gather as much information as you can about your audience's knowledge about the topic. Ask questions and take notes. Quickly try to organize this information in order to make a presentation based on what is already public. Be sure to separate facts from opinions, and avoid any speculation. Do not validate anyone's rumors by repeating them aloud—remind the audience that you deal with facts, not gossip.

2. Assure the audience that you are in control and that you are doing everything possible to address the situation. Use your personal and professional power to comfort the audience—you are involved and taking action.

3. Remember the techniques you learned for addressing troublesome questions in Chapter 14.

4. Keep in mind that when you say something publicly, it usually becomes a "fact." Be very careful when choosing your words—sometimes even when you repeat someone's question, it can be misconstrued that you are making a statement. Be sure to say, "What I have been asked is . . . ," or "What I hear you asking me is . . . ," before you repeat someone's question.

5. Keep away from any possible misleading words—the use of euphemisms or other terms to lower the impact of a message, or conditional language. Avoid such words as *may, could,* and *might.*

6. Keep it brief.

7. Never respond to a quote attributed to someone who is not present at the meeting. If someone asks you, "What do you think about what Mr. Smith said about this . . . ," reply that you will speak directly with Mr. Smith at a later time.

8. Do not use a student's, parent's, or teacher's name in a situation such as this.

9. Keep calm!

ACTING VERSUS PUBLIC SPEAKING

Since you are examining this kind of situation, this is an appropriate point to detail the difference between public speaking and acting. Acting assumes a suspension of disbelief about what goes on onstage. Your listeners are fully aware that they are sitting in uncomfortable seats in a crowded auditorium watching a performance. They are also fully aware that the humans on stage are portraying someone or something else, and yet the audience will factor in all of that and still suspend their normal levels of disbelief *if* the performance holds their interest. If the performance does not hold their interest and they no longer believe in it, they become keenly aware of the passage of time, the less-than-perfect comfort of the seats, and the man snoring down the aisle. Actors benefit from a proscenium arch over the stage, which, in a way, symbolizes the relationship the actors have with the audience. The actors customarily will not acknowledge that there is an audience watching them as they unfold their story. This is the kind of social contract between the actor and the audience that is present when acting is taking place.

Public speakers, in contrast, do not make use of a proscenium. Public speakers need to interact with their audience, and the success of their efforts relies heavily on their abilities to make eye contact and connect with their listeners.

In this case, however, the actor in you might need to speak out!

23

Using Appropriate Grammar

Much like knowing the ingredients to use in making a delicious cookie, it is important to know the basic elements or parts of speech to use when writing a good speech. While nobody assumes that you will become a grammarian, it still stands to reason that your speech should contain all of the proper parts in the correct order.

While there are several excellent books available on learning the elements of grammar, you will find below some of the fundamental or universal aspects of grammar, which you should have at your command as you begin to consider what to do should all else fail.

Parts of Speech

The Noun. As you know, a noun is a person, place, thing, or idea. There are two categories of nouns: proper or common and collective. *Proper nouns* are capitalized names of people, geographic locations, businesses, and so forth. These indicate that there is only one of a special kind of noun. *Common nouns* are the noncapitalized, regular things that fill the rest of the world. Collective nouns are singular nouns used to indicate a group of persons or things. They use a singular verb when the noun shows the group acting as one (e.g., The team *is* playing well today.). They use a plural verb when the noun shows members of the group acting individually (e.g., The team *are* playing different positions.). Hint: If you can plug in the word *members* before the verb, meaning that each member is doing something different, use the plural verb.

The Pronoun. A pronoun is a word that stands in the place of a noun. Remember: Pronouns always stand up for one another. There are many different forms of pronouns. A subjective pronoun is used in place of a noun as a subject of a sentence (e.g., The boy ran home . . . *he* ran home.). An objective pronoun is used in place of a noun in the predicate of a sentence (e.g., The boy hit the ball; the boy hit *it*.). Pronouns are used with all six parts of the verb *to be: I am; you are; he, she, or it is; we are; you are; they are.* There are also possessive pronouns that show possession (e.g., *my, your, his*). Reflexive pronouns end in *self* or *selves* (e.g., *myself, ourselves, herself*). Relative pronouns start adjective clauses. These pronouns are *that, which, who, whose, whom,* and *where.* The interrogative pronoun is used when asking questions: *who, whom, what,* and *which.* There are other forms of pronouns, but the last ones to discuss here are the demonstrative pronouns: *this, that, these,* and *those.* Be sure to use them as pronouns and not as adjectives (e.g., *This* textbook is great! In this example, *this* is an adjective. But *this* is great! In this example, *this* is a pronoun.).

The Adjective. This one is straightforward. An adjective modifies or portrays a noun or pronoun (e.g., A *red* ball is attractive.). For the record, the articles—*a, an,* and *the*—are also adjectives.

The Verb. The verb shows action in a sentence: *run, ran, hit, jump.* The verb also joins the subject of a sentence to its predicate, but more on that later. Do not forget the little words that help the verbs, the helping verbs: *am, is, has, could, be.* These helpers come before a verb (e.g., I *am running.*). Just when you thought you knew everything about verbs, here comes a twist. *Linking verbs* do not show action. A linking verb links, or glues, a noun or pronoun with its modifier adjective or noun. Think of an adjective such as *happy.* Imagine that you want to say that your friend is in a state of happiness. You could say *happy friend.* However, this does not sound very well educated. Instead, you could say, "My friend *is happy.*" In this way, you have linked the noun (friend) with its adjective (happy). In this example, *is* is the linking verb, and *happy* is called the predicate adjective, because it is an adjective, and it is in the predicate rather than coming before the noun it describes. Be careful with this one. If someone asks how you are *feeling,* and you say, "I feel *well,*" what you have really said is that your fingers have the capacity to sense pressure and heat to a high degree (*well* is an adverb). You should have said, "I feel *good,*" because *good* is an adjective modifying *I.* If someone asks, "What do you do for a living?" you could answer, "I am a *student.*" In this case, *student* is a noun telling what you are. This is called a *predicate nominative.*

The Adverb. An adverb is a word that modifies a verb, adjective, or another adverb. Most adverbs end in *ly*, such as *quickly*. Other adverbs are *soon, now,* and *too.*

Conjunctions. Simply put, conjunctions (*and, or, nor, but, for, yet*) join words and groups of words. They also join independent clauses with each other; in these cases, a comma comes before the conjunction.

Interjection. *No way!* Get it? It is a fast command or comment with no subject, usually followed by an exclamation point.

Putting It Together: Bigger Parts of Speech, Phrases, Clauses, and Sentences

The Preposition and Prepositional Phrase. The preposition is usually a small word that defines where or when something is happening. Some popular prepositions are *above, below, after, before, at, off, in, on, beside, between, down, during, until, since, through, to, up, on,* and *out.* There are many more examples. Prepositions usually do not stand by themselves; they usually begin what is called a prepositional phrase. A basic phrase is a group of words that do not have a verb on board, such as *in the car, before the game,* or *under the cat.*

If a phrase begins with a preposition and ends with a noun or pronoun, it is a prepositional phrase: *in the backyard* is a prepositional phrase. It begins with a preposition and ends with a noun. The noun or pronoun is referred to as the object of the preposition. Prepositional phrases are used as big adjectives or adverbs. In other words, a prepositional phrase acts just the way an adverb or adjective would. Watch this phrase: *in the backyard.* In the sentence, "Let's play *in the backyard,*" the prepositional phrase modifies the verb *play;* therefore the whole phrase is a big adverb, called an adverb phrase. In the sentence, "The boy *in the red coat* is happy," *in the red coat* is an adjective phrase because it acts like an adjective. Try this: "The boy in the red coat is happy to play in the backyard." How many prepositional phrases can you find?

The Other Phrases. You do not want to spend a great deal of time on *verbals,* but you should be aware of their existence. Look first at a gerund and gerund phrase.

■ A *gerund* is a verb that thinks it is a noun in context (e.g., *Running* is fun.). As you can see, if you did not know about a gerund, you would have a very hard time explaining that what looks like a verb ending in *ing* is actually a noun. When you start a phrase with a gerund and end it with an object, you have a gerund phrase: gerund plus object (*Running the park* is fun.). Be careful. You can be fooled here. For example, what about this sentence: "Running *in the park is fun.*" Is that a gerund phrase? No. *In the park* is a prepositional phrase, and *running* is a regular gerund.

■ A *participle* is sort of a mix between a verb and an adjective. Most participles end with an *ing, ed,* or *d.* Examples of a participle are *a running boy* or *a crying baby.* The participle phrase then follows a familiar pattern, acting just like an adjective: participle plus object (e.g., *Removing his hat,* Bob sat down).

■ An *infinitive* is a form of verb that starts with the word *to.* Examples are *to run, to sleep,* and *to dream.* An infinitive can be used as a noun or as a modifier (adjective or adverb). As a noun: "*To forgive* is divine." As an adjective: "The time *to play* is near." Essentially, if a noun comes before the infinitive, it probably acts like an adjective. If a verb comes before the infinitive, it probably acts like an adverb. If nothing comes before the infinitive, it probably acts like a noun. An infinitive phrase is very tricky to spot. It begins with an infinitive and completes a thought with other modifiers or nouns (e.g., We want *to watch the game* as soon as possible.).

Appositives. Appositives are nouns describing other nouns, set off by commas (e.g., Bob, *the letter carrier,* is nice.).

The Sentence. A sentence contains a noun and verb plus maybe a direct object or indirect object, and maybe a few other modifiers. Just remember this: Your basic sentence has one noun and one verb and maybe an object or two; everything else is just window dressing (also known as modifiers). A *direct object* comes after a verb and takes the action of the verb (e.g., I hit the *ball.*). The *indirect object* shows where or to whom the action happened (e.g., I threw *him* the ball.). If you are in doubt about which object is which, try removing the object and seeing if you can add the preposition *to* in front of it. In "I threw *him* the ball," you can switch the sentence to say, "I threw the ball *to him*"; therefore, *him* is the indirect object.

Dependent and Independent Clauses. Just like a sentence, all clauses have a noun and a verb. There are some clauses that can stand alone and some that cannot. Independent clauses can stand alone (e.g., *You are running.*). Dependent clauses cannot stand alone (Tell us *what you said.*). Notice both still have a noun and a verb. Now that you have a basic understanding of clauses, examine how they act as big adjectives, adverbs, and nouns.

■ The **infinitive clause** contains an infinitive (*to*) and verb plus a subject (e.g., I asked *Bob to vote* for me.). *Bob to vote* cannot stand alone; therefore, it is what kind of clause?

■ The **adjective clause** starts with a relative pronoun (you remember, *that, which, where, who* . . .) plus a noun and a verb that together act like an adjective (e.g., The story *that you told* was great). *That you told* cannot stand alone; therefore, it is what kind of clause?

■ The **adverb clause** starts with a subordinating conjunction (*because, since, unless* . . .) plus a noun and a verb that act like adverbs (e.g., *Because you study public speaking*, you will be world famous.).

■ Finally, **noun clauses** begin with indefinite relative pronouns, which look identical to relative pronouns (*that, what, who, whom*) plus a verb and maybe a noun or a pronoun (e.g., Tell us *what you said.*). One way to discover if you have a noun clause instead of an adjective clause is to remove the clause from the sentence. If the sentence loses its original sense, it is just like taking a main noun out of a sentence. On the other hand, if you remove an adjective clause, it is just like taking a mere modifier out of a sentence—nothing fundamentally changes.

Voices. If the subject *verbs* the object, then it is in the *active voice*. For example, "*I hit the ball.*" Subject (*I*) verb (*hit*) the object (ball). On the contrary, if you said, "The *ball was hit* by me," then the subject (*ball*) verb (*was hit*) prepositional phrase (*by me*), and the sentence is in the *passive voice* because the person doing the action is not the subject of the sentence. When creating your speech, try to avoid using the passive voice unless you are trying to make a specific point. There are four main types of voices or purposes of a sentence: the interrogative, the imperative, the exclamatory, and the indicative (or declarative). The interrogative sentence asks a question and ends with a question mark. The imperative issues a command and may end with an exclamation point. The indicative simply states a fact or idea and ends with a period. The subjunctive sentence usually contains the verb *were* and indicates that the subject wishes or dreams about something.

Example
Speeches
and Additional
Supports

24

Three Sample Speeches

This chapter comprises three speeches that serve as examples: (1) A Graduation Speech, (2) How to Adopt a Hallway, and (3) Role-Play Exercise—Terror at 10,000 Feet.

A GRADUATION SPEECH

Good morning and welcome to our graduation. Mr. Smith and members of the board of trustees, Mr. Jones and fellow teaching colleagues, parents, grandparents, brothers and sisters, friends, students, and, of course, the students of the hour, our graduates.

We have gathered this morning to both acknowledge and celebrate the achievement of an important milestone in the lives of these young people during their lifelong journeys of self-discovery.

I would like to take this opportunity behind this bully pulpit to say a personal thanks to all of you who have touched our lives. I am not going to mention you by name, but I suspect that you have much the same feeling as I do right about now.

This is a class whose identities intertwined early on, and since then, they have been one of the tightest, most supportive groups I have ever seen move through a school. Now, it has not been all sweetness and light among the students. Believe me, there have been some spirited discussions about weighty matters over the years. On the other hand, if someone from outside the class has in any way imperiled any member of this group, I have never seen a collection close its ranks so quickly, which speaks well for their esprit de corps.

You in this class have studied together, you have played together, and you have grown together. Your years were filled with the wonders and joys of discovering who you are, what your bodies and minds are capable of doing and becoming, and what a complicated yet dazzling set of trials and errors life can be. Those of us who have had the excellent good fortune to work with you share in your reveling; we draw our own professional strength from your overabundant pools of energy, courage, and, sometimes, sheer tenacity.

As we prepare to deliver these young people on to the next level, I must say, of all of the life skills one could achieve in preparation for the new millennium, the ability to work with others in a cooperative-team fashion is the most critical. I am very happy to report that this group seems to have a good head start.

Together you came, you saw, and you did a darn good job. You have made our school the best.

It has been a distinct pleasure to have known you these past four years; you have my finest wishes for everything.

How to Adopt a Hallway

The Smith School is deciding if it wants to make plans to ensure that our hallways and stairs are free from trash. Following the model from the department of transportation, we are deciding if we want our own Adopt-a-Hallway plan. One part of our group believes that when the students take responsibility for their own learning environment, they will have a better appreciation for the necessity of keeping it clean. In this way, it's not someone else's problem, it is their own.

Under such a program, students are instructed that if they see a piece of paper on the floor on their designated watch, they should stop and pick it up and dispose of it properly. It should also be said that this does not mean it is okay to toss paper on the floor; it is everyone's responsibility to take pride in our school. As it is now, when teachers, principals, and school administrators see students picking up paper, we all congratulate them, and, in turn, we act as good role models ourselves by picking up papers. On the other hand, one part of our group feels that most students will not pick up paper unless they are watched constantly, and that would take more effort than having the maintenance staff keep the hallways clean as they now do.

ROLE-PLAY EXERCISE—TERROR AT 10,000 FEET

In this exercise, you and each of your colleagues should choose one of the following occupations to role-play. You can develop other occupations to add to this list, but you can use this file for starters:

- A banker
- A medical doctor
- A lawyer
- A veterinarian
- A sailor
- A mechanic
- A professional wrestler
- A writer
- A teacher
- A scientist
- A cook
- A soldier
- A young child
- An airline attendant
- An armed security officer
- A wealthy businessperson

- A meteorologist
- A college student

Once you have chosen your occupation, take a few minutes to develop your character. Picture in your mind what your character looks like and sounds like. Once you have this image in your mind, pretend that you are that person and try to answer some of these questions:

- What is your name?
- Where do you live?
- How old are you?
- Do you have any relatives?
- How often do you exercise?
- How sympathetic are you?
- How do you react in a crisis situation?
- How honest are you?
- How naive are you?
- How wealthy are you?

The Story's Skeletal Outline

You are a passenger aboard a small, twin-propeller airplane that is flying unhurriedly from New York City to Yarmouth, Nova Scotia. You are on your way to a conference on effective communication skills. The flight is mainly over water, although you do see tiny dots of islands from time to time as you cruise along on a sunny summer day. You have been in the air for several hours now, and the long flight is beginning to take its toll on your patience. You are tired and bored, and you want the flight to end.

You should always be careful what you wish for.

Suddenly, you hear a loud explosion, and the airplane takes a steep dive toward the water. After 30 seconds of screams and the reports of breaking glasses have filled your ears, the plane levels off—maybe a mile or two above sea level, according to your sight calculations. The pilot's voice comes over the public address system and reports that you have experienced just a little bit of choppy air and that everything would be back to normal "right quick."

"No reason to worry," you think to yourself.

Just then, the pilot and the copilot stroll casually down the center aisle each carrying a small toolbox. As they both disappear behind the dark curtain at the end of the fuselage, you relax, knowing that the situation is under control.

Three minutes later, your newspaper is blown off your serving tray as someone in the rear of the cabin shouts, "Hey, they're parachuting out the back of the plane!"

Several of the passengers race to the rear of the plane as you open the cockpit door. You cannot help but notice that while there was nobody in the command seats, the controls of the airplane were moving by themselves. "Autopilot," you say to yourself as you start checking the instruments. Everything seems all right, except for the altimeter that shows that the plane is flying at just below 10,000 feet adjusted for ground level and is dropping about 5 feet per second! You quickly calculate that at this rate, the plane will be bodysurfing in about 30 minutes.

When you race back to report this news to your fellow passengers, you hear that there are only four parachutes left onboard the plane, but at least they are the newer, static-line, square parachutes that, by opening automatically, increase the chances for survival—but they have to be opened by at least 3,200 feet to work. You recalculate that you now have approximately 20 minutes to make some tough decisions.

Your group will have to decide very quickly who is going to live through the impending disaster.

Exercise Procedures

These activities do not have to be completed in 20 minutes; that piece of information is included to heighten the sense of urgency in this scenario. To help you reach the best possible life-or-death decisions, you should follow these steps:

■ Based on your role-playing occupation, you and each of the other passengers have 1 minute or less to plead the case: Why should you get one of the parachutes? There should be no interruptions during the speeches.

■ After each person has spoken, you and each of the other passengers have 1 minute or less to confront any of the other passengers' spoken perceptions about themselves. Again, there should be no interruptions during the speeches.

■ When everyone has spoken, those whose characters were confronted have up to a 1-minute rebuttal each to defend themselves.

■ As an optional step to this exercise, following these speeches, you can allow 15 minutes for small-group and one-on-one discussions. During this time, you and your fellow passengers should be in contention with each other for your lives. Can your character form any alliances to guarantee your survival? Can your character make any believable promises that would be to the benefit of the others once you are on the ground?

■ When you are ready to continue, everyone takes a sheet of paper and lists four occupations (not names) that should receive a parachute. Tally the votes for all the occupations, and list the top six on a blackboard. The six people playing these occupations should come to the front of the room and take turns rolling two dice. The four people with the top totals of the combined dice will receive the parachutes and will live to tell the story another day.

Follow-Up Activity

As a group, discuss each person's speech to survive, each person's rebuttal, and each person's confrontation of the others. Did each speaker use problem-solving strategies that made sense in the given scenario? How would each person's occupation be more or less influential if a new scene took place in a hospital, or a police station, or even in your school?

Resource A: An Audience Evaluation Form

Please complete this form and return it to the speaker—thanks!
Please feel free to add any additional comments on the back of this
sheet.

Please circle the word(s) that best describe(s) your reaction:

(1) Speaker Preparation. I felt that the speaker was prepared
for today's presentation.

strongly agree ———————— agree ———————— strongly disagree

Comments:

(2) Quality of Audiovisuals. I felt that the speaker presented a
good mix of quality audiovisuals including handouts, overhead images, and computer displays.

strongly agree ———————— agree ———————— strongly disagree

Comments:

(3) Usefulness of Information. I feel that this is information that I can put to use. I feel that I had enough background information to appreciate what was presented here today.

strongly agree ——————— agree ——————— strongly disagree

Comments:

(4) Continuing Information. I would be interested in more speeches such as this in the future to learn more about topics such as these.

strongly agree ——————— agree ——————— strongly disagree

Comments:

Resource B:
The Hub
and Web
Worksheet

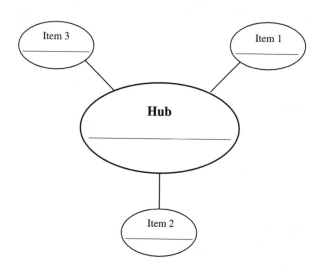

Glossary:
Definitions
of Terms Used
in This Book

adrenal glands. A group of cells or tissue located near the kidneys, which release natural chemicals to stimulate the heart and body.

adrenaline. A powerful, natural heart stimulant.

adrenocorticotrophic hormone (ACTH). A natural hormone that stimulates the cortex of your adrenal glands via the endocrine system, which in turn produces natural corticosteroids.

alliteration. Repetition of initial sounds in words that follow each other.

allusion. A reference to a topic or well-known person or place in your speech.

articulation. The physical makeup of the voice, or a clear statement of educational intent.

assonance. Repetition of vowels, change of consonants in a sentence.

back step. Lowering one's maturity level in response to a negative comment from a member of the speech study group.

caesurae. Strategic pauses in a speech.

clues. Nonverbal messages telling the speaker how well the speech is progressing.

circular language. See *recursive*.

consonance. Repetition of consonants, change of vowels in a sentence.

corticosteroids. Natural chemicals in your body that induce a fight-or-flight reaction during a speech.

critique. A formal or informal assessment of a speech.

Demosthenes. An outstanding Greek orator in 351 B.C. who, among other things, learned proper public-speaking techniques by first speaking with stones in his mouth.

denouement. Tying up any loose ends at the conclusion of your story.

escape. To Whom It May Concern: deny reality and ignore valuable comments about your speech.

extemporaneous speech. A brief speech about a given topic with little or no time to prepare.

fight or flight. The body's urge to run or fight rather than speak.

hidden agendas. Implied messages under the surface meaning of a speech or critique.

hub. The webbed center of your speech-focusing statement.

hyperbole. Overstatement.

hypothalamus. The part of the brain that triggers the defense reaction.

idea cards. Index cards used to sort topics and information.

impromptu speech. An off-the-cuff speech.

interpersonal communication. The term used for human communications.

irony. The use of words to express the opposite of what one really means.

juxtaposition. Opposite ideas placed side by side to create a new truth.

kinesthesis. Total physical makeup of the body.

leaks. Subconscious slips when under pressure.

malapropism. Verbal slip.

metaphor. Comparison not using *like* or *as*.

mnemonics. Mental tricks or devices to aid memory.

noradrenaline. A powerful, natural heart stimulant.

onomatopoeia. Making words from sounds, such as *boom* or *crash*.

paralinguistics. The way humans inflect words to produce certain meanings.

parody. Exaggerated imitations designed to make a point.

personification. Giving human characteristics to nonhumans.

projection. Placing the blame for a poor speech elsewhere; also, speaking so everyone in the room can hear you.

proxemics. The strategic use of physical space.

psychosomatic stress. The bodily reaction to speechmaking.

rationalization. Explaining away a poor speech.

recursive. See *circular language.*

reflection. Restating the speaker's message to avoid misunderstandings.

repression. "Forgetting" negative comments.

rhetoric. The proper use of language.

rubric. A written assessment that uses specific criteria to improve a speaker's confidence.

salutation. An opening greeting to an audience.

satire. An original, sarcastic speech usually based on human vices.

scan. Looking over an audience for five seconds before and after speaking.

segue. An immediate transition using various techniques.

shift. Transition in storytelling.

simile. Comparison using *like* or *as*.

speech-focusing statement. The heart of your introduction, which details the topics you will be covering, in order, during your speech.

speech study group. A supportive group of your colleagues that meets to discuss how to write and evaluate speeches and performances.

spoonerism. Unintentional transposition of the first sounds of two words in a sentence.

tone. The quality of your vocal sounds in a speech, and the verbal, figurative language you use to create an effect.

understatement. Stating less than reality.

> *Wise counsels may accelerate, or mistakes delay it; but sooner or later, the victory is sure to come.*
>
> —Abraham Lincoln, 1858

Index

**CORWIN
PRESS**

The Corwin Press logo—a raven striding across an open book—represents the happy union of courage and learning. We are a professional-level publisher of books and journals for K-12 educators, and we are committed to creating and providing resources that embody these qualities. Corwin's motto is "Success for All Learners."